THE 101 BEST

Saltwater Fishes

Cover Photographs by Scott W. Michael
Front: Maroon Clownfish
(*Premnas biaculeatus*), page 71
Back: Top - Longnose Butterflyfish (*Forcipiger flavissimus*), page 66
Middle - Cooper's Anthias (*Pseudanthias cooperi*), page 183
Bottom - Coral Hind (*Cephalopholis miniata*), page 106

Produced and distributed by:
T.F.H. Publications, Inc.
One TFH Plaza
Third and Union Avenues
Neptune City, NJ 07753
www.tfh.com

THE 101 BEST

Saltwater Fishes

HOW TO CHOOSE & KEEP HARDY, BRILLIANT, FASCINATING SPECIES THAT WILL THRIVE IN YOUR HOME AQUARIUM

Text & Photography by

Scott W. Michael

MICROCOSM

tfh

PROFESSIONAL SERIES™

A MICROCOSM EDITION

WWW.MICROCOSM-BOOKS.COM

DEDICATION

To my remarkable sisters, Sandy and Suzie.

Sandy took me to diving lessons and

aquarium stores before I could

drive, while, for a couple of summers,

Suzie let me use her Houston garage

as a lab for dissecting

sharks and keeping shrimp eels.

ACKNOWLEDGEMENTS

Many professional aquarists, committed home aquarists and fish wholesalers have assisted me greatly over the years and in preparing this book. I express immense gratitude to the following: Bob Pascua (Quality Marine), Bill Addison, Mitch Carl, Dr. Bruce Carlson, Millie, Ted, and Edwin Chua (All Seas Marine), J. Charles Delbeek, Tom Frakes, Kevin Gaines, Kyle and Mark Haeffner (Fish Store Inc.), Richard Harker, Jay Hemdal, Larry Jackson, Kelly Jedlicki, Kevin Kohen (liveaquaria.com), Morgan Lidster (Inland Aquatics), Chandra Liem (Golden Generation), Martin A. Moe, Jr., Bronson Nagareda, Alf Jacob Nilsen (Bioquatic Photo), Michael S. Paletta, Richard Pyle, Dennis and Erik Reynolds (Aqua Marines), Greg Schiemer, Frank Schneidewind, Mike Schied, Terry Siegel, Julian Sprung, Vince Rado (Oceans, Reefs and Aquariums), Wayne Sugiyama (Wayne's Ocean World), Leng Sy (Ecosystem Aquariums), Dr. Hiroyuki Tanaka, Takamosa and Miki Tonozuka (Dive and Dives), Jeffrey Turner (Reef Aquaria Design), Jeff Voet (Tropical Fish World), Tony Wagner (CaribSea), Randy Walker (marinecenter.com), Fenton Walsh, Jim Walters (Old Town Aquarium) and Forrest Young and Angus Barnhart (Dynasty Marine Associates).

I am extremely appreciative of the work of the Microcosm team, especially Alesia Depot, Kathleen Wood, Susie Forbes, Mary Sweeney, Judith Billard and Editor James Lawrence. Thanks also to the folks at T.F.H. Publications, especially Glen S. Axelrod, Mark Johnson, Chris Reggio, and George Rutz for helping this effort come to fruition.

Thanks also to my American and my New Zealand family for their support over the years. Anyone that knows me, knows that Janine Cairns-Michael, my wonderful spouse, is a saint who puts up with my obsessive-compulsive tendencies. Her never-failing support for nearly a quarter of a century has been essential for much of what I have achieved in my life.

—*Scott W. Michael*
Lincoln, Nebraska

CONTENTS

*Common Lionfish (*Pterois volitans*), page 113*

Using This Guide 9
Introduction 12

Marine Fishkeeping
Essential Husbandry for New & Intermediate Aquarists
Stocking Your Aquarium...............................16
Model Community Tanks 28
Foods & Feeding 160
Keeping Your Fish Healthy 170
Troubleshooting.......................................182

101 Best Saltwater Species 38
A Field Guide to Hardy Aquarium Species
Angelfishes 41
Anthias 51
Assessors 55
Blennies 56
Butterflyfishes 61
Cardinalfishes 67
Clownfishes 70
Comet 74
Convict Blenny 75
Damselfishes 76
Dartfishes...84

CONTENTS

Dottybacks 86
Filefishes 93
Firefishes 94
Gobies 96
Grammas 103
Groupers & Sea Bass 104
Hawkfishes...108
Jawfishes 112
Lionfishes 113
Moray Eel..115
Porcupinefishes 116
Rabbitfishes 117
Sandperches..118
Soapfishes 119
Tangs (Surgeonfishes) 120
Triggerfishes..123
Wrasses 128

Species to Avoid
The Big, The Bad & The Ill-fated............................142

Back Matter
Scientific Name Index..184
Bibliography...187
Common Name Index 188
Glossary 190
Credits 191
About the Author 192

Meant as a field guide to marine aquarium species, this guide uses color photographs taken in home aquariums as well as on coral reefs for quick visual identification. Species appearing here have been selected as outstanding for their hardiness and durability in aquarium conditions, for their attractiveness and interesting behaviors.

Fishes are arranged alphabetically by common name within their family groupings.

In addition to a species overview and notes about aquarium behaviors and compatibility, each account contains concise facts and advice, organized as follows:

COMMON NAME

In this guide one or more common names are listed for each species. The first name provided is the name most frequently used in the authoritative checklists and field guides written by ichthyologists. In assigning the preferred common name to each species, I have attempted to steer away from obvious misnomers and toward names that will minimize confusion and bring science and hobby closer together.

SCIENTIFIC NAME

This is the most-current name applied to the fish by the scientific community. The name is in the form of a binomial. The first name indicates the genus to which the fish belongs, while the second is the species name. When common names are confusing, the scientific name is a benchmark that all can understand. For example, Amphiprion ocellaris is the scientific name for a much-liked reef fish that goes by all of these common names: Ocellaris Clownfish, Common Clownfish, False Percula Clownfish, Clown Anemonefish and others. The genus name often provides a clue to the traits and keeping requirements of other closely related species grouped within that genus.

MAXIMUM LENGTH

This indicates the greatest length that an individual of that particular species can attain—or the longest ever reported—measuring from the end of the snout to the tip of the tail. In most cases, the length of an aquarium specimen will fall short of this measure, but the aquarist should always plan for the prospect of his or her fish reaching a maximum length close to that presented.

NATIVE RANGE

This entry notes the broad geographical area where each species occurs. The distribution of a fish is of great value to aquarists wishing to set up a tank that represents a natural community or biotope from a certain geographical region.

MINIMUM AQUARIUM SIZE

This is the minimum suitable aquarium volume for an adult individual of the species. Of course, juveniles and adolescents can be housed in smaller tanks. Activity levels and behavior patterns of a particular species have been accounted for whenever possible. Please note that bigger aquariums are almost always better for most species. (The exception being very tiny fish that tend to be lost in large tanks.) The suggested sizes given throughout this book must be regarded as the minimum, and providing more space will allow any fish to acclimate better and display less aggression toward its tankmates.

FEEDING

Marine fishes vary dramatically in their feeding preferences and requirements. Advice in this section includes the type of foods generally preferred by the species. Daily feeding frequency is recommended.

Meaty foods for carnivorous fishes include: fresh or frozen seafoods (e.g., shrimp, scallop, squid, mussels, clams, marine fish flesh); dried and frozen aquarium foods, including mysid and brine shrimp, krill, marine plankton, worms of various types, anchovy-like silversides, and others. High-quality prepared rations may also contain sea urchins, sea worms, and other high-protein marine ingredients that are relished by many fishes. A number of prepared frozen foods are specially formulated for angelfishes (sponge-feeders), sharks and rays, triggerfishes, and others.

Live foods include: adult or newly hatched brine shrimp, mysid (or *Mysis*) shrimp, grass shrimp, black worms, feeder fish and many other items from pet and bait shops.

Herbivore foods include: dried and frozen preparations that contain unicellular algae (especially *Spirulina*) and various types of red, green, and brown marine algae. Many aquarists feed table vegetables, such as spinach, zucchini, broccoli, or even carrots. (These are usually microwaved, blanched, or frozen and thawed before feeding.) The sushi-wrap sheets of nori also make excellent fare for herbivorous marine species.

Color enhancers are now recommended for many, if not all, marine aquarium species. An increasing number of marine rations contain added vitamins and pigments, such as carotenoids, to help maintain the fish's natural bright colors.

Live rock and live sand are indicated as important sources of food for some species. Many protozoans, crustaceans, worms, and micro- and macroalgae reproduce on and within such natural substrates, and these will supplement the diet of many fishes.

HABITAT

Many marine fishes will do best in aquariums aquascaped to replicate the portion of the reef they inhabit in the wild. Some need deep sand substrates to thrive, many others only acclimate well when provided a profusion of rocky caves, overhangs, bolt holes and hiding places in the reefscape to provide them a sense of security. Having the proper habitat is a major stress reliever for most coral reef fishes.

The art & science of picking the right species for your aquarium

What a wonderful time to be a marine fishkeeper! I have been keeping and studying coral reef fishes, both in aquariums and in the wild, for more than three decades and have never seen such a profusion of species of fishes and invertebrates available to home aquarists. Never before have we had such an amazing assortment of aquarium equipment, excellent new fish foods and valuable information—and never before have so many people worldwide kept thriving saltwater aquariums in their homes and offices.

At the same time, the incredible diversity of species making their way into retailers' tanks can be overwhelming at times. How to choose among them? The fact is, there are many, many fishes sold that are not easy to keep or that have special feeding or care requirements that the average hobbyist may not be willing or able to meet. In fact, some of the fishes you are bound to see for sale in local fish shops or online are virtually impossible to maintain for long, even by experts. Sorting through this ever-changing, ever-beguiling swarm of species and determining which are likely to survive, and which are not, can be a daunting task for the inexperienced fishkeeper.

FISH THAT THRIVE

One well-known secret in the aquarium trade is that losing a favorite fish (or a whole tankful) is a major reason why many people become discouraged and give up on their aquariums. In my own case, I can remember all-too-well acquiring a Mandarin Dragonet for my first 20-gallon tank. I knew nothing about this odd creature, but was intrigued by its glorious, multi-colored "coat" and its droll behaviors. The store where I bought it did nothing to dissuade me from taking on what I now know is a very finicky little fish. The results of my first Mandarin experience were not good—within a month the dragonet was dead, and my 12-year-old heart was broken. If I had not been so crazy about reef fishes, I might have aban-

Sailfin Tang: a classic survivor and great aquarium fish for larger tanks.

doned my new hobby and gone back to assembling plastic models of planes and army tanks. Premature fish loss is something we all want to avoid.

For the last 30 years I have been keeping detailed records of the fish I have had in my care in my own aquariums and at the pet stores I have worked in, managed and owned. In assembling and writing six previous books on marine fishes, I have also gathered a trove of valuable data on species husbandry and behavior from hobbyists and professional aquarists around the world who have been willing to share their experiences, successes and failures with different fishes.

It is my hope that this book will make life easier for new and intermediate hobbyists, livestock sellers and aquarium maintenance professionals. This book is meant to help users match the right fish with the right keeper—a challenge that is easier said than done.

NEED-TO-KNOW FACTS

In my days as a marine fish retailer, as well as a partner in an aquarium maintenance company, I would often encourage customers to look at books and come up with a list of fishes that they wanted to keep in their "slices of captive ocean." Invariably, they would select at least some species that were clearly unsuitable–fishes that would be difficult to feed, prone to disease, or that were sure to grow too large for their home aquariums.

It was too often a chore trying to talk to the hobbyist who had his or her heart set on purchasing a Blue Ribbon Eel, a Flame Fairy Wrasse or a Moorish Idol they had seen while perusing a picture book on reef species. This was the genesis of the idea for *The 101 Best Saltwater Fishes.* If I had had the facts in a book like this, it could have saved so many of my customers and me much time and headache during the all-important species-selection process.

So how did we select the 101 "best" species? The fishes included were picked for several different reasons, but the overarching criterion was that the fish be hardy and easy to keep. In addition, we gravitated to the species that are attractive and/or interesting aquarium residents and that are relatively easy for any local fish store to acquire. There are certainly other species that could be included, but I wanted to narrow the choices to make the selection process as

Mandarinfish: stunning but very likely to starve without expert care and feeding.

clear and simple as possible for neophytes (as well as hobbyists needing to restock or make a fresh start).

I also feel that many aquarists can benefit from having some up-to-date general husbandry guidelines and advice. We have included chapters and practical tips on creating balanced fish communities in different size tanks, on foods and feeding, health matters, and troubleshooting.

Some controversy is sure to surround the section on *Species to Avoid.* Many sellers of livestock cringe when they see a list of fishes that hobbyists should not keep, but I feel the marine hobby needs to be responsible and steer uninformed buyers away from inappropriate choices. Most of the fishes on my "red list" are difficult to keep for one or more reasons, while others just get way too large and/or too active for all but the most immense home tank. While this species list may change as new foods and husbandry techniques evolve, there is no doubt that the fishes in this section should be reserved for only the most experienced marine aquarists.

Finally, I believe that the fishkeeper who starts with the recommended species will be more likely to meet with success and the satisfaction of having a healthy, vibrant marine aquarium. As you gain experience with these more durable aquarium residents, you will become better prepared to take on other more challenging and undeniably alluring coral reef species.

How to mix and match fishes in a balanced marine community

Most potential dog owners—or at least the prudent ones—spend some time researching the breed or breeds they are thinking about buying. If you've ever owned or paged through a book on canine puppies and breeds, you know they usually have a sizeable chapter on selecting the "right dog" for your specific lifestyle.

I only wish that more marine fishkeepers were as thoughtful when choosing new species for their aquariums. Given the right conditions, a coral reef fish can easily live as long as a puppy, perhaps even longer. With reasonable care, many can live more than 10 years, and 20 years is not unheard of. If you are good at picking the right fish, it can become a long-term member of your household. Doing a bit of initial research before bringing home a new fish can prevent many of marine aquarium keeping's most predictable headaches and heartbreaks.

A SEA OF CHOICES

Walking into a fish store with a large marine fish section can be mind-boggling if not downright intimidating—there is so much variety! Not only do these fishes display an amazing array of body shapes and color schemes, many may differ in their behaviors, their natural ecology, and their captive requirements.

For example, some of the fishes available to us are highly territorial or so predatory in the wild that they will wreak havoc in a tank full of smaller or milder-mannered species. Pick a species with these instincts and you may see the rest of your fish collection battered or even eaten by the new tankmate.

With a profusion of species, the coral reefs of the world provide modern marine aquarists with a mind-boggling and growing array of stocking choices.

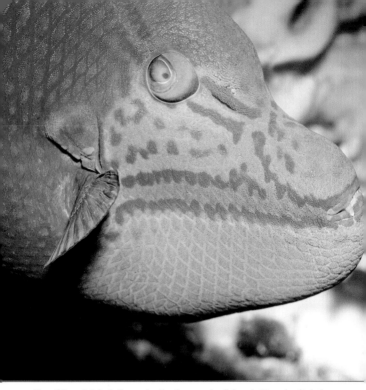

Niger Triggerfish hails from a family of aggressive fishes, but knowing its behavorial profile will allow the aquarist to fit it into certain fish communities.

Then there are fish species so shy that you'll be lucky to see them once they are introduced to a tank full of live rock and myriad hiding places. Choose unwisely and these furtive or passive fish may hide constantly and fade slowly away from starvation and stress.

Feeding is a highlight of the day when keeping a marine aquarium, but some fishes require two or even three or more meals daily to stay healthy. Others have very specific diets that can be time-consuming, expensive or impossible to provide. Some species need lots of swimming room, while others must have a deep layer of sand to burrow into. Finally, there are also marine fishes available at your local pet store that are destined to grow huge and overwhelm any home aquarium.

To create a balanced, beautiful, interesting marine system, the thinking aquarist will need to be aware of the profile and husbandry needs of each fish before making a purchase and adding a new fish to his or her tank.

PLANNING YOUR FISH COMMUNITY

So where do you start in planning a fish community and finding out about species-specific traits and care requirements? The first step is to make a list of the species that you are interested in keeping—ideally, you do this even before you purchase the aquarium or before you start to re-populate an existing tank. Look through this and other reference books with good profiles of marine aquarium species or take a notebook to your favorite fish store and jot down the names of all the species that you find interesting. I would cast a wide net. Write down any fish that strikes your fancy. As you build your list, put an asterisk by those species that you want the most. I call these "the must-have species."

Now the real research begins. For each species, you need to fill in a few vital blanks. Start with books, online aquarium

---

MARINE SPECIES PROFILER

1. HOW LARGE DOES THIS SPECIES GET? When it reaches adulthood, will it fit into the tank you intend to set up?

2. HOW AGGRESSIVE IS IT? What sort of tankmates might it harm?

3. WHAT DOES IT EAT? Does it have specific dietary requirements that will be difficult to meet or does it have a generalized diet?

4. IS IT PISCIVOROUS (a fish eater) or will it graze on the choice invertebrates you want to keep, such as ornamental shrimp, corals or clams?

5. WHAT ARE ITS HABITAT PREFERENCES? Is it a fish that demands lots of space? Does it have any special aquascaping requirements?

6. IS IT SUSCEPTIBLE TO DISEASE?

7. IS IT CONSIDERED EASY OR DIFFICULT TO KEEP? Do you have the skills (and resources) to be sure it has a chance to thrive?

---

news groups, and the staff at reputable local fish stores. I have provided a short list of questions that you should try to answer about each species in the Marine Species Profiler on page 19. You will also want to get some idea how difficult it will be to get the fish on your list and how much they might cost.

In narrowing your choices, you may find that you want to build a captive fish community around one of your "must-have species." For example, if one of the asterisked fish is very aggressive, you may have to limit your fish collection to other aggressive fishes or larger fishes that your pugnacious center-piece fish is more likely to ignore. For example, if your key species happens to be a grouper or lionfish, you will have to choose tankmates that are too large for it to swallow. If, on the other hand, your aquarium world must revolve around a beautiful group of Flasher Wrasses, small and/or peaceful tankmates will be required. Some species are either so aggressive or so easily intimidated that they deserve to have a whole aquarium dedicated to their special needs. For most newcomers and intermediate fishkeepers, a mix of compatible species makes the most sense.

HABITAT CONSIDERATIONS

One benefit to having a stocking plan is that your final fish selections may influence the way you set up and aquascape the tank. It may also have some bearing on the size and shape of the tank you purchase. For example, if I decide I cannot live without one of the large, active species, such as the French Angelfish, I will need to provide enough swimming room to accommodate its size and need to roam. This may mean keeping the décor to a minimum, selecting a tank with more surface area or a larger tank than originally planned. If one of the most important fish on my list likes to spend its time on or burrowing in the substrate, I will need to have some open sand bottom so it can do what comes naturally. If I keep species with pugnacious tendencies, I need to provide plenty of hiding places—rocky caves and niches—for all of my charges.

After doing the research, your list has been whittled down considerably. Now, if you are planning a new system,

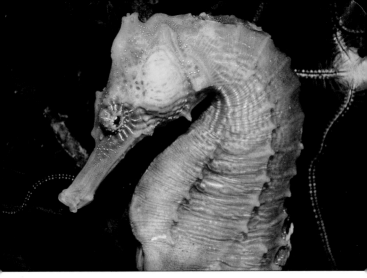

Although beautiful and beguiling, this Common Seahorse has special needs, including frequent feedings of high-quality and live foods to survive.

put the species in order from least aggressive to most aggressive. This is very important, because you will want to add the least aggressive fishes to your tank first, and the most pugnacious species last. In ranking fishes by disposition and relative aggressiveness, a number of variables come into play: how a fish acts will depend on the size of the tank, the size of the fish compared to its tankmates, the number of hiding places available, what other species are being kept, and even the number of times a fish is fed a day will have some impact on how it behaves. There will also be that freak individual that breaks all the rules set for its species. Remember, fish don't read the books—what makes them interesting is that they don't always do what the literature says they will. The disposition ranking is only a rough guide for a particular species.

STOCKING DENSITY

There are a number of variables that will determine your tank's fish-carrying capacity. Using live rock, protein skimmers, and other modern filtration methods, we can more efficiently keep nitrogenous waste products at bay. More often than not, behavioral factors will limit the number of fish in a tank. Space and hiding places are usually the limiting factor today in many fish-only aquariums. When you overcrowd your

*Juvenile Koran Angelfish (*Pomacanthus semicirulatus*) can grow by leaps and bounds in a single year, demanding that the aquarist plan for its full adult size.*

tank, aggression (and the resulting stress and disease outbreaks) becomes a more acute problem than the carrying capacity of the biological filters. Of course, an overcrowded aquarium can lead to deteriorating water quality (declining pH and the build-up of dissolved organic wastes and nitrate) as well. All of these factors can make fish more susceptible to disease, listlessness, color loss and other ailments. Therefore, it is always better to have one or two fish too few, with a small but healthy margin for error.

Predicting the appropriate stocking limit of a tank can be tricky and is often more art than science. Many equations have been proposed to enable you to find the carrying capacity of a tank's biological filtration. But these "inch-per-gallon" equations have inherent problems. First of all, the mass of the fish, not the length will determine the amount of waste that it produces. A hefty 6-inch grouper is going to produce more waste than a pencil-thin 6-inch moray. Secondly, the metabolic rate also varies from one species to the next. Active wrasses and anthias, for example, are going to consume more food and produce more waste than a slow-moving comet. Food consumption, and associated waste production, is also likely to be greater for a younger fish than an adult.

As we develop our fish communities, we must also allow

room for growth. Under favorable conditions, your reef fish will grow quickly. A Koran Angelfish may be just two inches long when you acquire it, but it can easily triple its size in a year's time. Unless you plan on buying a larger tank to accommodate growing fish, you need to put together your community for adult fish, not the juveniles that most of us start with. Yes, the tank may look somewhat empty initially, but the fish will grow to fill the space with astonishing speed.

ADULT SIZE FACTORS

Predicting the maximum size your fish will reach in captivity can be difficult. A Queen Angelfish, for example, can reach a maximum of 18 inches in the wild, but few attain this top size. Larger species more often than not only attain 75 to 90 percent of the maximum length recorded, while smaller fishes (grammas, dottybacks, fairy wrasses, flasher wrasses, gobies, blennies) regularly come close or reach the proposed maximum sizes listed in the reference tables.

So—how many fish can you realistically expect to keep in your 75-gallon tank? Here are some rules from other published "experts:" one inch of fish per 2-5 gallons of tank; 2 gallons per medium-sized fish (2 to 3 inches or less in length); six to eight fish, no bigger than 3 or 4 inches, for every 27 gallons of water; 1 medium-sized fish per 10 gallons of water. According to the most conservative of these equations, you could keep seven or eight, three-inch fish in your 75 gallon tank, while the most liberal allowances suggest that you could go with over 30 fish that are two to three-inches in length.

Bewildered? I suggest a number somewhere toward the lower estimate, perhaps 12 to 14 small to medium-sized fish, or about two fish per each ten gallons of tank capacity. Once again, remember that tank size and biological filtration are not the only things to consider. You also need to think of behavioral factors and the types of fish going into the aquarium. See pages 28-37 for some balanced fish communities that can fit into a range of tank sizes. If you do regular maintenance, have good biological filtration, and aquascape as suggested, these communities can be successfully maintained with minimal risk of serious aggression between tankmates or losses due to predatory behaviors.

PACING YOUR POPULATION PLAN

To my mind, the most important thing when stocking your tank is to go at it slowly and enjoy the process. It should be at least six months before you reach your aquarium's carrying capacity.

The worst mistake I see is trying to reach the population apex as fast as possible. During a stint in the aquarium retail business, I witnessed attempts to do this on a number of occasions—usually the "grand opening" of a new home or business. Disaster (for the living specimens involved, as well as the owners' pocketbooks) was the result in almost every case. There is a saying among veteran aquarists: "Nothing good ever happens fast in a marine aquarium."

Those who scuba dive will also be very familiar with the mantra: "Plan your dive and follow your plan." The same applies in stocking a marine aquarium. Have a concept for your aquarium and stick to it. Inevitably, a great fish will appear in a local shop and unexpectedly catch your eye, but I urge you to ask the basic questions and learn about its behavior and husbandry requirements before bringing it home. Somehow each new fish must fit with the overall scheme for the aquarium community you are creating.

If you find that the species in question has a tendency to be more boisterous, it should be added into the tank only after the less aggressive species have had a chance to settle in. Because we need to take our time when adding fish to our aquariums, you may have to wait to purchase this new fish until more of the species on your list are added to the tank. Other opportunities will come along. Be aware that spontaneous, uninformed purchases can scuttle the best of stocking plans and can come back to haunt you. "I HAD to have that triggerfish," is one recent admission I heard from a well-heeled hobbyist. "The next morning I found he had eaten my whole collection of *Tridacna* clams." Fatter by hundreds of dollars worth of clam flesh, the trigger had to be returned.

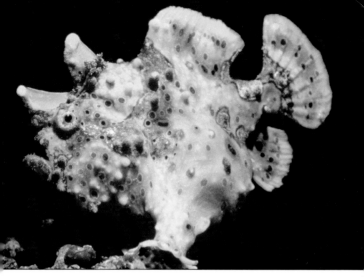

So cute but worth a second thought: a Clown or Warty Frogfish may catch the fish buyer's eye, but it is capable of eating all the smaller fishes in a tank.

Know when to stop. When you reach your tank's carry-capacity you don't purchase more fish. Restraint is not easy, and I know this from personal experience. Buying a new fish is undeniably exciting, but self-discipline is important when it comes to buying any live animal. Succumbing to the temptation to add just one more fish to a fully stocked aquarium can jeopardize everything you have accomplished. Always populate a tank with the future growth of the species you purchase in mind.

Of course, if your fish are outgrowing their space or you have absolutely no room for new species, you have a great excuse to start thinking of setting up a new, larger system.

AGGRESSION—IMPORTED FROM THE REEF

Behavioral stress, usually caused by one or more irascible tankmates, can cause long-term problems in a fish community. Many reef fishes naturally stake out and defend only a limited territory in the wild, and they are typically not indiscriminately aggressive. They display antagonism towards members of their own species and other fishes that compete with them for shelter or food and they recognize competitors by their shape, color and behavior.

When a fish is collected for the aquarium trade, it brings all this behavioral baggage along and into its new aquarium home. Our task as marine fishkeepers is to manage or curb these aggressive tendencies. We do this by carefully selecting the types of fish that we put together, by introducing the fish into the tank in a logical order and by making sure there are enough necessary resources—most importantly, hiding places and food—to go around.

There are a number of factors that determine how one fish may behave toward another species in captivity. There are species specific differences. That is, some species have a greater propensity to be aggressive than others. There is the case of prior residence. If an individual has been in a tank for a while, it is more likely to be aggressive to a newcomer. A fish is also more likely to behave aggressively if there is a lack of space and shelter. If these valuable resources are in short supply, tank occupants will fight to acquire and keep them. Finally you must consider the physical and behavioral characteristics of the potential aggressor's tankmates.

As mentioned above, reef fish do not indiscriminately attack other fish, but recognize competitors. Studies have shown the most important recognition cue is body shape, with individuals displaying more antagonism toward species with similar body plans. Body shape, to some degree, is an indicator of diet. The majority of herbivores are deeper-bodied and laterally compressed, while most predators are more elongate. Therefore, it makes sense for a fish to chase away species with the same form, because they probably also have a similar diet.

Color is also an important recognition cue. A study carried out on captive butterflyfishes indicated that species with similar color patterns were more aggressive towards one another than they were to those that differed chromatically.

Finally, the feeding behavior of a species can make it susceptible to attack. At least one damselfish identifies competitors by how they feed. If an approaching fish is grazing along in a characteristic herbivore manner, nipping at the substrate, a resident damsel will attack it and drive it from its territory.

CURBING AGGRESSION: TRICKS & TACTICS

Several approaches and tricks can be followed to help control aggression toward incoming specimens:

- ADD THE LEAST-AGGRESSIVE FISH SPECIES FIRST and the most belligerent last.
- DO NOT OVERCROWD your aquarium. More space per fish equals less aggression. That said, in some cases, crowding certain fish species, such as anthias, can reduce the likelihood that any one fish is harassed to death.
- PROVIDE PLENTY OF FUNCTIONAL HIDING PLACES.
- BREAK UP AQUARIUM AQUASCAPING into numerous smaller rocky mounds rather than one larger one if you have a larger tank.
- AVOID KEEPING CONSPECIFICS OR CLOSELY RELATED SPECIES in the same tank, especially if the tank is small.
- AVOID KEEPING SIMILARLY SHAPED OR COLORED species, particularly if one of them is known to be aggressive.
- TURN OFF THE LIGHTS when introducing a new fish.
- FEED RESIDENT FISH FIRST before adding a new fish.
- REARRANGE AQUASCAPING before adding new fish.
- PLACE THE FISH IN A CLEAR CONTAINER, like a plastic gallon jar with holes in it, or partition off a portion of the tank with a clear piece of acrylic, and let the residents grow accustomed to the new introduction for several days or more before removing it from the enclosure.
- ADD A SMALL MIRROR TO THE AQUARIUM to divert some of the resident fishes' aggression.
- ISOLATE THE AGGRESSOR FOR SEVERAL DAYS in a quarantine tank and then reintroduce it when the new fish is established.

2-GALLON (8 L) NANO-REEF AQUARIUM

1 Neon Dottyback	*Pseudochromis aldabraensis*

Like others in the family, the Neon Dottybacks are ideal for nano-reef tanks because they remain small, are colorful, and are often too aggressive to keep in smaller tanks with other fishes. Provide a small cave for the fish to hide in.

5-GALLON (19 L) NANO-REEF AQUARIUM

1 Blackray Shrimp Goby (w/ shrimp)	*Stonogobiops nematodes*
1 Firefish	*Nemateleotris magnifica*

Here is a fascinating pairing of a Blackray Shrimp Goby and its snapping shrimp partner (usually Randall's Snapping Shrimp, *Alpheus randalli*). The shrimp is a serious excavator so provide a sturdy reef structure such as a flat piece of rock for it to burrow under. The Firefish provides color and activity higher up in the water column.

12-GALLON (45 L) NANO-REEF AQUARIUM—WESTERN PACIFIC

1 Redbanded Shrimp Goby (w/ shrimp)	*Amblyeleotris fasciata*
1 Purple Firefish	*Nemateleotris decora*
1 Yellow Assessor	*Assessor flavissimus*

This little reef is home to a shrimp goby paired with a Tiger Snapping Shrimp (*Alpheus bellulus*). Provide a 4-inch bed of sand with bits of shell and rubble, with rocky sheltering places for the other fish.

12-GALLON (45 L) NANO-REEF AQUARIUM

1 Neon Goby	*Elacatinus oceanops*
1 Yellowhead Jawfish	*Opistognathus aurifrons*
1 Royal Gramma	*Gramma loreto*

The industrious jawfish will require a 4-inch deep sand bed, with sand and shells of varying grades to assist burrowing. The Royal Gramma needs a suitable hole to shelter in, as will the Neon Goby. It is likely you will be able to watch the goby clean its tankmates.

Queen Angelfish: the focal-point species for a larger tank, page 48.

Yellow Clown Gobies in a thicket of coral—perfect for a nano-scale reef tank.

20-GALLON (76 L) PEACEFUL AQUARIUM—GOBIES/BLENNIES

2 Sailfin Blenny	*Emblemaria diphyodontis*
1 Purple Firefish	*Nemateleotris decora*
2 Yellow Clown Goby	*Gobiodon okinawae*
1 Blackray Shrimp Goby	*Stonogobiops nematodes*

This tank is home to a variety of gobies and blennies. You can watch the pair of sailfin blennies interact, while the firefish and shrimp goby will spend time in the water column. A small, faux branching coral makes an ideal hangout for the Yellow Clown Gobies.

20-GALLON (76 L) PEACEFUL AQUARIUM—WESTERN PACIFIC

1 Firefish	*Nemateleotris magnifica*
1 Canary Fang Blenny	*Meiacanthus oualauensis*
1 Redbanded Shrimp Goby	*Amblyeleotris fasciata*
2 Unarmed Perchlet	*Plectranthias inermis*

Add both Unarmed Perchlets at the same time —making sure one is smaller than the other. The shrimp goby (and preferably a partner shrimp) will require a small cave or crevice at the base of the reef structure, as will the Firefish. The bright yellow Canary Fang Blenny will spend most of its time cruising all levels of the aquarium.

20-GALLON (76 L) PEACEFUL AQUARIUM—"MIXED"

2 Yellowstriped Cardinalfish	*Apogon cyanosoma*
1 Tailspot Blenny	*Ecsenius stigmatura*
1 Royal Gramma	*Gramma loreto*

This aquarium is for the non-purist who doesn't mind mixing species from different oceans. The Tailspot Blenny loves to back into small holes in the live rock, while the cardinalfishes need a crevice or cave in which to take refuge if startled. The Royal Gramma is the odd-fish-out—a resident of the tropical Atlantic while the others are from the Pacific—but it is colorful and ideal for smaller tanks.

55-GALLON (209 L) SPECIES AQUARIUM

1 Picasso Triggerfish	*Rhinecanthus aculeatus*

Featuring the personable Picasso Triggerfish, this is a classic species tank. Provide this piscine pet with a crevice in which to scoot into when startled and at night, as well as numerous bits of shell and rubble bits. The trigger will put on a show, constanting rearranging its aquascape and acting as the bold ruler of its domain.

55-GALLON (209 L) PEACEFUL AQUARIUM—WESTERN PACIFIC

2 Yellow Assessor	*Assessor flavissimus*
2 Pajama Cardinalfish	*Sphaeramia nematoptera*
1 Golden Wrasse	*Halichoeres chrysus*
1 Falco's Hawkfish	*Cirrhitichthys falco*

Here is a community of relatively mild-mannered reef fishes from the Western Pacific. The pair of Yellow Assessors, which will need a cave or overhang to call home, must be added to the tank simultaneously. The pair of Pajama Cardinalfish should spend most of their time in the open, but provide them with a crevice or branching coral for refuge. The Golden Wrasse will provide color and movement and will need a fine sand bed to burrow in. The small Falco's Hawkfish has the potential to be a bit bossy and should be added to the tank last after the others have established their own territories.

75-Gallon (285 L) Peaceful Aquarium—Caribbean

3 Yellowhead Jawfish	*Opistognathus aurifrons*
2 Chalk Bass	*Serranus tortugarum*
1 Blue Chromis	*Chromis cyanea*
1 Swissguard Basslet	*Liopropoma rubre*
2 Royal Gramma	*Gramma loreto*

The chromis, Chalk Bass, and Royal Gramma provide color and activity throughout the tank, while the jawfishes will spend their time near the aquarium bottom (provide them with a sand bed at least 4 inches deep). The Swissguard Basslet tends to be more secretive, and needs a cave or rocky crevices where it will lurk in security.

75-Gallon (285 L) Peaceful Aquarium—Western Pacific

2 Unarmed Perchlet	*Plectranthias inermis*
2 Ocellaris Clownfish	*Amphiprion ocellaris*
3 Yellowstriped Cardinalfish	*Apogon cyanosoma*
1 Midas Blenny	*Ecsenius midas*
1 Longnose Butterflyfish	*Forcipiger flavissimus*

The tiny Unarmed Perchlet pair should be provided with suitable hiding places, while the clownfish can be kept with a host sea anemone, if the tank has strong lighting and water movement. Haddon's Sea Anemone (*Stichodactyla haddoni*) is a hardy species often accepted by this species in captivity. Add two small, captive-raised clownfish. The blenny and butterflyfish add color and movement to the scene.

Swissguard Basslet is a prize fish for a Caribbean peaceful community tank.

90-Gallon (341 L) "Mixed" Aquarium—Indo-Pacific

3 Zebra Dartfish	*Ptereleotris zebra*
2 Ocelarris Clownfish	*Amphiprion ocellaris*
1 Yellow Shrimp Goby	*Cryptocentrus cinctus*
2 Yellowtail Damselfish	*Chrysiptera parasema*
1 Ornate Wrasse	*Halichoeres ornatissimus*
1 Lyretail Hawkfish	*Cyprinocirrhites polyactis*
1 Pacific Doublesaddle Butterflyfish	*Chaetodon ulietensis*

This community consists of a selection of relatively peaceful to slightly aggressive Indo-Pacific species. The group of Zebra Dartfish will provide lots of action and fascinating behavior to observe—they need suitable holes and crevices at the base of the reef for hiding. The Yellow Shrimp Goby can be paired-up with a suitable snapping shrimp. The damsels could cause behavioral problems in a smaller tank, but should be fine in a tank of this size with the species recommended. The Ornate Wrasse will need a fine sand bed to bury in, while the hawkfish and butterflyfish will increase the amount of activity in the tank. (See the 75-gallon (285 L) Western Pacific tank opposite for more information on keeping the clownfish pair.)

100-Gallon (380 L) Predator Aquarium—Indo-Pacific

1 Snowflake Moray Eel	*Echidna nebulosa*
2 Zebra Lionfish	*Dendrochirus zebra*
1 Common or Volitans Lionfish	*Pterois volitans*
1 Carpet Eel Blenny	*Congrogadus subducens*
1 Bluechin Triggerfish	*Xanthichthys auromarginatus*

Here is a fish community for the aquarist drawn to more voracious pets. For authenticity and to provide a sense of security to this collection of hunters, be sure to furnish plenty of rocky shelter, in the form of live rock canyons and caves, for the moray eel, Zebra Lionfish, and the Carpet Eel Blenny. As the "focal species" in this tank, the Common Lionfish will grow large with magnificent finnage and will need open swimming space. There are several jumpers in this group, so a secure top is mandatory.

135-Gallon (513 L) "Mixed" Aquarium—Western Pacific

6 Bartlett's Anthias(1 ♂ : 5 ♀)	*Pseudanthias bartlettorum*
2 Pajama Cardinalfish	*Sphaeramia nematoptera*
1 Redfin Fairy Wrasse	*Cirrhilabrus rubripinnis*
1 Longnose Hawkfish	*Oxycirrhites typus*
1 Longnose Butterflyfish	*Forcipiger flavissimus*
2 Longfin Bannerfish	*Heniochus acuminatus*
1 Bicolor Blenny	*Ecsenius bicolor*
1 Sixline Wrasse	*Pseudocheilinus hexataenia*

Comprised of a careful balance of peaceful and moderately aggressive fish species, this a very lively tank. The group of colorful anthias will provide a cloud that drifts about the aquarium. (Be sure not to add more than one male anthias, or non-stop battles will ensue.) The cardinalfish pair, fairy wrasse, Longnose Butterfly and bannerfish are also active species and their colors/color patterns will add eyecatching interest. The hawkfish, blenny and Sixline Wrasse will slink or hop about the bottom, giving the tank interest at all levels. There are a number of accomplished leapers in this community so be sure you have the tank covered.

Longnose Butterflyfish adds interest to a Western Pacific community tank.

135-GALLON (513 L) MODERATELY AGGRESSIVE AQUARIUM—WESTERN PACIFIC

1 Coral Beauty Angelfish	*Centropyge bispinosus*
1 Halfblack Angelfish	*Centropyge vrolikii*
1 Tomato Clownfish	*Amphiprion frenatus*
1 Sailfin Tang	*Zebrasoma veliferum*
1 Harlequin Tuskfish	*Choerodon fasciata*
1 Arc-eye Hawkfish	*Paracirrhites arcatus*
1 Niger Triggerfish	*Odonus niger*

This is a beautiful collection of bolder, self-assured species. Add the two pygmy angelfish at the same time to reduce the likelihood of aggression and be sure they have plenty of hiding places. You can include a host sea anemone (preferably a captive-bred Bubbletip Sea Anemone, *Entacmaea quadricolor*, which is quite hardy) for your Tomato Clown if you have good light and water movement. The tang will need lots of open swimming space. The tuskfish is a true focal fish—the bold orange bands and protruding baby blue fangs will grab any viewer's attention. Both the hawk- and triggerfish should be added to the tank after all others are well-acclimated.

Harlequin Tuskfish is bold, colorful and less menacing than it appears.

180-GALLON (684 L) AGGRESSIVE AQUARIUM—"MIXED"

1 Foxface Rabbitfish	*Siganus vulpinus*
1 Maroon Clownfish	*Premnas biaculeatus*
1 Pinktail Triggerfish	*Melichthys vidua*
1 Bird Wrasse	*Gomphosus varius*
1 Yellow Tang	*Zebrasoma flavescens*
1 Coral Hind	*Cephalopholis miniata*
1 Queen Angelfish	*Holacanthus ciliaris*

This aggressive community tank is comprised of some truly spectacular fishes. It is imperative that the tank contains plenty of larger hiding holes as well as ample swimming space. If you have good lighting over the tank and plenty of water movement, you could include a captive-bred Bubbletip Sea Anemone (*Entacmaea quadricolor*) for the clownfish. Try to acquire a smaller Coral Hind. (If the hind can ingest any of its fish tankmates, it will.) A Queen Angel of around 3 to 5 inches will acclimate more readily than a larger adult.

180-GALLON (684 L) "MIXED" AQUARIUM—INDIAN OCEAN

1 Auriga Butterflyfish	*Chaetodon auriga*
1 Klein's Butterflyfish	*Chaetodon kleinii*
2 Clark's Clownfish	*Amphiprion clarkii*
1 Indian Yellowtail Angelfish	*Apolemichthys xanthurus*
1 Yellowbar Angelfish	*Pomacanthus maculosus*
1 Neon Dottyback	*Pseudochromis aldabraensis*
1 Niger Triggerfish	*Odonus niger*
1 Purple Tang	*Zebrasoma xanthurum*

Two of the stars in this interesting gathering of personalities are the angelfishes. Provide them with suitable hiding places, as well as room to cruise. The clownfish can be housed with some of the more durable sea anemones—a Bubble Tip (*Entacmaea quadricolor*), Corkscrew Tentacle (*Macrodactyla doreensis*) or Haddon's Sea Anemone (*Stichodactyla haddoni*). There is one problem: the butterflyfishes that may attempt to eat the anemone. That said, it is likely that the pair of clownfish will defend their host.

180-Gallon (684 L) "Mixed" Aquarium—Red Sea

6 Bluegreen Chromis	*Chromis viridis*
1 Midas Blenny	*Ecsenius midas*
6 Lyretail Anthias (1 ♂ : 5 ♀)	*Pseudanthias squamipinnis*
1 Orchid Dottyback	*Pseudochromis fridmani*
1 Springer's Dottyback	*Pseudochromis springeri*
3 Longfinned Fairy Wrasse (1 ♂ : 2 ♀)	*Cirrhilabrus rubriventralis*
1 Yellowbar Angelfish	*Pomacanthus maculosus*
1 Purple Tang	*Zebrasoma xanthurum*

Here is a dream fish community from the Red Sea. It includes two dottybacks that are endemic to this area. The shoal of chromis will provide plenty of motion to this active aquarium. The Lyretail Anthias tends to be a more aggressive species—it is imperative that you include just one or else a single male and group of females. There is also a trio of fairy wrasses (keep only one male with a couple of females). With all three of these species, all individuals in the group should be added simultaneously. Be sure the aquascape has a profusion of hiding places, caves and rocky grottoes and canyons.

Male Lyretail Anthias is a showstopper but can be kept only with a number of females of the species. It will fight incessantly with another male.

A field guide to aquarium fishes: species that can thrive for you

For the marine fish enthusiast, bringing home a new fish—one that a matter of days before might have been swimming on a remote coral reef in Fiji, Hawaii, Australia or the aquamarine waters of the Caribbean is one of life's pulse-quickening moments.

To be sure that you are not bringing home a bag full of trouble or a fish that has little chance of surviving in a typical home aquarium, the following 101 species are presented as great choices, especially for less-experienced marine aquarists—or those who want to improve the odds that their new acquistions will thrive.

For simplicity, the species are arranged in alphabetical order by common name of the family or group—Angelfishes, Butterflyfishes, Cardinalfishes, and then by common name of each species.

COLOR KEY TO SIZES

One of the most important criteria for selection of a fish is its eventual adult size. Will it fit in your aquarium? Will it be an appropriate tankmate for your other fishes or fishes you plan to buy? The cute baby grouper that can grow into a foot-long, greedy predator that eats all your prized clownfish and small wrasses may not be the best choice.

Here is the Size Key used in this guide:

> SMALL (or NANO)
> Requires minimum aquarium size of 10-30 gal. (38-114L)

> MEDIUM
> Requires minimum aquarium size of 50-75 gal. (190-285L)

> LARGE
> Requires minimum aquarium size of 100-180 gal (380-684L)

The Yellowtail Damselfish is a popular and hardy choice for beginning hobbyists but picking the right damsel requires some research and foresight.

STOCKING SLOWLY

One word of warning: Wherever you buy your fish, don't acquire too many at any one time. It is often tempting to load-up on livestock when you drive some distance to buy fish or order from a mail-order fish supplier. Some impulsive fish shoppers can't handle having so many choices at their finger tips and end-up with more fish than they can safely introduce at one time. The problem is that quarantine space is often limited. This means you'll end-up crowding fish in your quarantine tank or, even worse, introducing them directly into the display tank because of space limitations. Either situation all too often ends in disaster. You will be better able to monitor and treat one or two individuals (or a school of a single species) at a time in your quarantine tank, rather than five or six different fish.

Finally, to my mind, buying a fish sight-unseen is a questionable practice, unless you use a known, reputable supplier. I much prefer to see what I am getting in a local shop and, perhaps, paying a little more. "THINK GLOBAL, BUY LOCAL" is not a bad rule in today's wired world, and it holds especially true in buying live aquarium fish.

LOOKING BEFORE LEAPING

I like to encourage aquarists to take their time in selecting a new fish from a dealer's tanks. See a fish you particularly like? Here's a quick checklist of things to ask and watch for before making the decision to buy it.

3 QUESTIONS: A FISH-BUYER'S CHECKLIST
Things to consider before bringing home a new fish

1. IS THE SPECIMEN you are watching alert, clear of wounds or signs of disease (white spots, patches of unhealthy skin or fins).
2. IS THIS FISH EATING? (If in doubt, ask them to feed the fish and be sure that it has a healthy interest in food.)
3. HOW LONG has the dealer had the fish? (If it has just arrived, you may want to have them hold it for a few days or a week to be sure it recovers from the stresses of shipping.)

CHERUB ANGELFISH *Centropyge argi*
(Atlantic Pygmy Angelfish)

MAXIMUM LENGTH: 3.1 in. (7.9 cm).
NATIVE RANGE: Southern Florida, Bahamas, Caribbean.
MINIMUM AQUARIUM SIZE: 30 gal. (114 L).
OVERVIEW: This is a gorgeous little fish with electric-blue highlights and a bold attitude that belies its size and common name.
FEEDING: Omnivore. Feed a varied diet of meaty and algae-based foods at least twice a day. In a well-established reef tank with abundant grazing opportunities, feeding once a day may be sufficient.
HABITAT: Reef, often in areas with coral rubble and/or macroalgae. Provide plenty of rocky hiding places—crevices and caves.
COMPATIBILITY: This fish can be a real hellion, especially in a smaller aquarium, and it is best not to house it with peace-loving fishes, such as flasher wrasses and firefishes. In a nano-size tank, it may have to be kept singly; two or more can be housed together in a large aquarium. Two males together will fight until one succumbs. Females tend to be smaller than males, otherwise the sexes do not differ in color. It tends to be one of the better angelfishes to keep with corals, although it will occasionally go to the dark side and pick at xeniid soft corals, large-polyped stony corals, mushroom anemones and clam mantles.
AQUARIUM BEHAVIOR: The Cherub Angel is active and fascinating to watch, spending much of its time moving from one shelter site to the next, grazing on algae when it feels safe. It will spawn in captivity, but the larval young need special feeding and care to survive.

CORAL BEAUTY *Centropyge bispinosa*
(Two-spined Angelfish)

MAXIMUM LENGTH: 3.9 in. (10 cm).
NATIVE RANGE: Indo-Pacific.
MINIMUM AQUARIUM SIZE: 30 gal. (114 L).
OVERVIEW: This is an excellent beginner's angelfish, having both eye-catching beauty and an ability to adjust and do well in many home aquariums. Its colors vary considerably, with orange, purple or blue hues predominating in fish from different regions.
FEEDING: Omnivore. Feed meaty and algae-based foods several times a day. Will benefit from the presence of some live algae for grazing and regular supplementation with color-enhancing marine rations.
HABITAT: Reef. Provide various sheltering places in the form of caves and crevices in the live rock aquascape.
COMPATIBILITY: While the Coral Beauty may be antagonistic toward passive species introduced after it has acclimated to its new home, it is typically not overly combative. More than one can be kept in the same tank if it is large enough and the fish are added simultaneously. Add two smaller individuals or one large and one small to decrease chances of getting two males, which are more likely to quarrel with each other. As with all the smaller angelfish species, an occasional individual may nip at large-polyped stony corals or clam mantles.
AQUARIUM BEHAVIOR: This can be a rather shy species that peeks out from hiding places, occasionally moving out from cover to pick at detritus and algae on the aquarium substrate. It will be bolder in a peaceful community setting.

FRENCH ANGELFISH *Pomacanthus paru*

MAXIMUM LENGTH: 15 in. (38 cm).

NATIVE RANGE: Tropical Atlantic, Caribbean.

MINIMUM AQUARIUM SIZE: 135 gal. (513 L).

OVERVIEW: This large, elegant fish is an icon of the Caribbean and has a reputation for surviving extremely well in captive systems. Observing the chromatic metamorphosis from black-and-yellow striped juvenile to handsome adult with gold-rimmed scales is a memorable experience for the fishkeeper.

FEEDING: Omnivore. Feed meaty and algae-based foods several times a day. Will graze on algae. Frozen sponge-based angelfish rations may be eaten with relish.

HABITAT: Reef or reef-sand interface. Provide it with several bolt holes and plenty of open swimming space.

COMPATIBILITY: This species is not overly aggressive, but can be somewhat rowdy in certain venues. It will occasionally chase smaller, passive species, but usually does not harm tankmates if space is not in short supply. It is best to add less aggressive species before it. Keep only one per tank, unless you have a very large system and can acquire a pair. It is risky to keep this fish with clams, large-polyped stony corals and some soft corals.

AQUARIUM BEHAVIOR: Juvenile French Angelfish have bold personalities and are well-known for their cleaning behaviors in the wild. The young fish will perform a fluttering swimming display to attract potential clients—including large snappers, surgeonfishes and even moray eels—to be groomed of parasites and other unwanted attachments.

HALFBLACK ANGELFISH *Centropyge vrolikii*
(Halfblack Pygmy Angelfish, Pearlscale Angelfish)

MAXIMUM LENGTH: 4.7 in. (12 cm).
NATIVE RANGE: Eastern Indo-West Pacific.
MINIMUM AQUARIUM SIZE: 55 gal. (209 L).
OVERVIEW: With subtle coloration highlighted by bright-orange eyeliner, this is an attractive fish and one of the more durable smaller angels. Its color is mimicked by the Chocolate Surgeonfish (*Acanthurus pyroferus*) and it will commonly hybridize with several other pygmy angel species.
FEEDING: Omnivore. Feed a variety of meaty and algae-based foods at least twice a day—perhaps less where lots of algae growth is present.
HABITAT: Reef, coral rubble zones and/or sandy lagoon areas with macroalgae. Provide plenty of places where it can hide.
COMPATIBILITY: This fish is not overly pugnacious, but has been known to chastise newly added fishes that are smaller or more mild-mannered. If you plan to keep it with these types of fishes, add the angel to the tank last and be sure there are plenty of places for it to hide. The Halfblack Angelfish can be kept in pairs, or if the tank is large enough (e.g., 180 gallons [684 L]), it is possible to keep a group. It is imperative to keep only one male, as they will fight incessantly. Males tend to be larger than females. It is not a great risk to corals, but like many in the genus may go astray and begin nipping at xeniid soft corals, large-polyped stony corals and clam mantles.
AQUARIUM BEHAVIOR: The Halfblack Angelfish will dash from one hiding place to another, inspecting the substrate for algae or detritus on which to graze.

INDIAN YELLOWTAIL ANGELFISH *Apolemichthys xanthurus*
(Smoke Angelfish, Cream Angelfish, Xanthurus Angelfish)

MAXIMUM LENGTH: 5.9 in. (15 cm).

NATIVE RANGE: Western Indian Ocean.

MINIMUM AQUARIUM SIZE: 75 gal. (285 L).

OVERVIEW: This species is a great choice for novice angelfish keepers. While not the most flamboyant member of the family, the Indian Yellowtail is a commendable mid-size angelfish and certainly one of the hardiest.

FEEDING: Omnivore. Feed a variety of meaty foods, dry and frozen rations with algae and sponges at least three times a day.

HABITAT: Reef or reef-sand interface. Provide plenty of swimming room for this fish.

COMPATIBILITY: This is a fairly passive species for an angelfish. It may occasionally pick on smaller fishes added after it is established in the tank, but it lacks the scrappiness of some members of the family. It is best to keep only one per tank, as they are likely to quarrel with one another, unless you have a very large tank (180 gallons [684 L] or more), in which case you can keep a pair. It can be safely kept with some of the soft tree corals, but it has been known to irritate large-polyped stony corals.

AQUARIUM BEHAVIOR: While it may be shy initially, once aclimated to its new tank, the Indian Yellowtail Angelfish will become a bold, showy species. Be sure the aquascape provides bolt holes—that is, large caves or crevices into which it can dart when frightened.

KORAN ANGELFISH *Pomacanthus semicirculatus*
(Semicircle Angelfish, Halfcircled Angelfish)

MAXIMUM LENGTH: 13.8 in. (35 cm).

NATIVE RANGE: Indo-West Pacific.

MINIMUM AQUARIUM SIZE: 135 gal. (513 L).

OVERVIEW: This is a survivor species, a regal but rugged aquarium fish that typically does well in larger home systems. This fish exhibits great color transformations as it grows. Juveniles are dark overall with white and bright-blue lines, while adults have a curving band of bright scales and hot-blue highlights.

FEEDING: Omnivore. Feed meaty and algae-based foods several times a day. Will benefit from occasional meals of sponge-containing angelfish rations.

HABITAT: Reef. Provide ample open swimming space and several bolt holes in which shelter is readily available.

COMPATIBILITY: Keep one per tank, as they will fight. Juveniles will battle with any other angels having similar coloration. It can be quite cantankerous in a smaller tank. For this reason, it is a good idea not to house it with mild-mannered fishes or at least add the angel to the tank last. It is less likely to harm its neighbors if housed in a larger tank provided with many hiding places. Like other sizable angels, it is a potential threat to corals, especially as it becomes larger.

AQUARIUM BEHAVIOR: As a juvenile, it is relatively shy and will spend much of its time peering from a cave or crevice. As it increases in size, so too will its bravado ramp up in proportion. Adults tend to be very confident and smart and make wonderful pets.

LAMARCK'S ANGELFISH *Genicanthus lamarck*
(Swallowtail Angelfish, Blackstriped Angelfish)

MAXIMUM LENGTH: 9.1 in. (23 cm).

NATIVE RANGE: Indo-West Pacific.

MINIMUM AQUARIUM SIZE: 100 gal. (380 L).

OVERVIEW: This sleek, elegant fish is a member of an unusual angelfish genus that spends more time swimming high in the water column feeding on zooplankton than most others in the family. Because of its alternative lifestyle, it looks very different from its more robust kin.

FEEDING: Carnivore; plankton feeder. Offer meaty foods like frozen mysid shrimp and enriched brine shrimp at least three times a day.

HABITAT: Reef. Provide plenty of open swimming space, as well as rocky grottos and hiding places.

COMPATIBILITY: This species forms harems in the wild and can be kept in pairs or in trios (one male and two females). Lamarck's Angelfish males have jet-black pelvic fins; the females' are white, making it easy to select a male and female to keep together. If you keep more than one, be sure the tank is large enough—at least 135 gallons—to provide adequate swimming space. They are one of the least aggressive angelfishes, although adults may pummel small zooplankton feeders such as fairy wrasses, flasher wrasses, dartfishes and firefishes. It is one of the best angelfishes for a reef tank, but may occasionally nip xeniid and large-polyped stony corals.

AQUARIUM BEHAVIOR: This open-water angelfish spends most of its time swimming actively in the aquarium's upper spaces, providing constant movement to the reefscape.

QUEEN ANGELFISH *Holacanthus ciliaris*

MAXIMUM LENGTH: 17.7 in. (45 cm).

NATIVE RANGE: Tropical Western and Eastern Atlantic.

MINIMUM AQUARIUM SIZE: 180 gal. (684 L).

OVERVIEW: Big, beautiful and full of both grace and stout character, this is indeed the Queen of the angelfish family. However, it is not for everyone, as it gets large and will require lots of swimming room.

FEEDING: Omnivore. Feed meaty and algae-based foods several times a day. Will benefit from the presence of some live algae and sponge-enriched rations.

HABITAT: Reef or reef-sand interface. Provide one or more large bolt holes, rocky crevasses or caves for shelter.

COMPATIBILITY: It is best to keep only one Queen Angelfish per tank. The young will attack members of their own kind, but are usually not overly aggressive toward unrelated species. As they grow, they are not only antagonistic toward their kin, but they also become more belligerent, and may chase and nip more passive neighbors. A Queen Angel is a threat to a wide range of corals and ornamental invertebrates, and is not considered a desirable addition to the reef tank.

AQUARIUM BEHAVIOR: The juveniles will clean other fishes and often hover near the entrance of a crevice or cave. As they grow, they get more confident and spend more time roaming in the open. Once it recognizes its keeper as a source of food, it will beg at the tank surface and take food from his or her fingers. Try to acquire a healthy juvenile and watch it grow; adult angelfishes (of any species) can be hard to acclimate to a new aquarium setting.

WHITETAIL PYGMY ANGELFISH *Centropyge flavicauda*
(Pacific Pygmy Angelfish)

MAXIMUM LENGTH: 3.1 in. (7.8 cm).

NATIVE RANGE: Indo-Pacific.

MINIMUM AQUARIUM SIZE: 30 gal. (114 L).

OVERVIEW: Although not the most stunning of the small angel-fishes, this is a handsome little fish that endears itself to aquarists by its hardiness and its ability to thrive in smaller aquariums.

FEEDING: Omnivore. Feed meaty and algae-enriched foods at least twice a day or less in a tank where lots of live algae is present.

HABITAT: Reef, rubble and/or lush macroalgae. Be sure the aquas-cape has plenty of caves, crevices and sheltering holes.

COMPATIBILITY: Keep one per tank, unless you have a 75-gallon (285 L) tank or larger and you can acquire a male and female or two females. The sexes can be distinguished by color—males have short blue, horizontal bars on the rear margin of the dorsal and anal fins. Females lack these and tend to be smaller than males. If you intend to keep a pair, add them to the tank simultaneously. The Whitetail Pygmy Angelfish is usually not overly aggressive, although more peaceful fishes should be introduced before it. It is more likely to cause prob-lems with its tankmates in the tight confines of a smaller aquarium. It has been known to nip at fleshy coral polyps and clam mantles, but, if well fed, tends to do so less often than other angels.

AQUARIUM BEHAVIOR: This is a shy species that flits from one hid-ing place to another. It picks at the substrate, grazing diatoms and detritus off the aquarium rockwork and sandy bottom.

YELLOWBAR ANGELFISH *Pomacanthus maculosus*
(Yellowband Angelfish, Maculosus Angelfish, African Angelfish)

MAXIMUM LENGTH: 19.7 in. (50 cm).

NATIVE RANGE: Red Sea and western Indian Ocean.

MINIMUM AQUARIUM SIZE: 180 gal. (684 L).

OVERVIEW: This magnificent Red Sea angelfish is a real winner, a true presence in any aquarium and regarded by many as "bullet-proof"—impervious to variations in its captive environment. It is a personable aquarium inhabitant and exhibits stunning colors, but demands a larger system to accommodate its adult size.

FEEDING: Omnivore. Feed meaty and algae-based foods several times a day. It will benefit from the presence of some live algae for grazing.

HABITAT: Reef, with lots of swimming space. As with most angel-fishes, it acclimates best with one or two suitable bolt holes in the aquascape where it can dash into hiding.

COMPATIBILITY: Keep only one per tank, as they are likely to quarrel in most home aquariums. Juveniles will attack each other and similarly colored members of the family. This fish will not typically throw its weight around unless its tankmates are close relatives or they are added to a crowded tank after the angel has been in the aquarium for some time.

AQUARIUM BEHAVIOR: This lovely fish will spend most of its time cruising about the aquarium. It often becomes the dominant speci-men in a tank, but not at the expense of smaller tankmates. Captive-raised specimens are sometimes available and highly recommended.

BARTLETT'S ANTHIAS *Pseudanthias bartlettorum*
(Christmas Island Anthias)

MAXIMUM LENGTH: 3.5 in. (8.9 cm).
NATIVE RANGE: South Pacific.
MINIMUM AQUARIUM SIZE: 55 gal. (209 L).
OVERVIEW: Anthias are undeniable eye-catchers in the marine aquarium, with beautiful coloration, a habit of swimming constantly in the open water column, and a total disinterest in eating or harming corals or other invertebrates. This is one of the hardiest choices among the many anthias that are collected.
FEEDING: Carnivore; zooplankton feeder. Offer meaty foods such as frozen mysid shrimp, enriched adult brine shrimp, squid or marine plankton at least three times a day. Regularly include color-enhancing foods in its diet to ensure that it maintains its glorious colors.
HABITAT: Reef environment with plenty of hiding places. Does best in clean, highly oxygenated aquariums with plenty of swimming room and lots of water movement.
COMPATIBILITY: While groups of anthias make showy additions to the reef tank, it is important to add just one male and to keep them in groups of six or more (e.g. five females and one male). Add all individuals at once. May be bullied by larger, more aggressive species (dottybacks, hawkfishes, damselfishes). It may pick on diminutive zooplankton-feeders in a smaller tank.
AQUARIUM BEHAVIOR: This is a wonderful reef species that will spend most of its time dashing about in the water column. A dominant female may eventually transform into a male.

LYRETAIL ANTHIAS *Pseudanthias squamipinnis*
(Scalefin Anthias, Sea Goldie, Orange Anthias, Purple Anthias)

MAXIMUM LENGTH: 4.7 in. (11.9 cm).

NATIVE RANGE: Indo-West Pacific.

MINIMUM AQUARIUM SIZE: 55 gal. (209 L).

OVERVIEW: An icon of the coral reef, this anthias is ubiquitous in the Indo-Pacific, often forming large feeding shoals that hang as a brilliant curtain over current-prone reefs. It is one of the easier anthias to feed and keep in the home aquarium.

FEEDING: Carnivore; zooplankon eater. Feed meaty foods such as frozen mysid shrimp at least three times a day.

HABITAT: Reef. Provide ample open-water swimming space and brisk water flow to mimic their natural environment.

COMPATIBILITY: In smaller aquariums, it will fight with other anthias (it is one of the more aggressive members of the anthias clan). Keep singly unless you have a large tank—100 gal. (380 L) or more. While a shoal makes a lovely addition to a spacious reef aquarium, care must be taken in creating this assemblage. Add a single male and a half dozen or more females, introducing them simultaneously. (Males have a purple cast and an elongated ray streaming from their dorsal fin; females are orange.) Once acclimated, this species can be quite aggressive toward other zooplankton-feeders (e.g., dart gobies, fairy and flasher wrasses).

AQUARIUM BEHAVIOR: If kept in groups, the male will dart through his harem and occasionally chase females. In a large tank, if there are lots of females, one of them may change sex and begin competing with the resident male.

REDBAR ANTHIAS *Pseudanthias rubrizonatus*
(Redbelted Anthias, Redband Anthias, Tricolor Anthias)

MAXIMUM LENGTH: 3.9 in. (10 cm).

NATIVE RANGE: West Pacific.

MINIMUM AQUARIUM SIZE: 55 gal. (209 L).

OVERVIEW: This beautiful anthias often occurs in deeper water around wrecks and outer reef walls. It needs proper feeding and has a feisty disposition, making it best suited to communities of larger fishes that are not easily intimidated.

FEEDING: Carnivore; plankton feeder. Offer meaty foods, such as mysid shrimp and enriched brine shrimp, at least three times a day. It is prone to color and weight loss if not given a varied diet, and an ample quantity of food and pigment-enhancing rations.

HABITAT: Reef. Provide plenty of holes and crevices and good water movement.

COMPATIBILITY: This is a fairly pugnacious anthias. It is best to keep a solitary individual, unless you have a large aquarium (100 gal. [380 L] or more). To keep a group, it should consist of one male and six or more females. The males of this species are yellow posteriorly, have an orange head and a broad red bar on their sides. Females are light red with yellow marks on the scales and a white ventrum. It is also risky to keep this species with most other anthias species and peaceful zooplankton feeders, such as fairy wrasses and firefishes, in a smaller tank.

AQUARIUM BEHAVIOR: This fish will spend most of its time swimming in the open, but will dash for a hiding place if threatened.

UNARMED PERCHLET *Plectranthias inermis*
(Highfin Perchlet, Geometric Hawkfish, Hawkfish Anthias)

MAXIMUM LENGTH: 2 in. (5 cm).

NATIVE RANGE: Indo-West Pacific.

MINIMUM AQUARIUM SIZE: 10 gal. (38 L).

OVERVIEW: This attractive little fish is ideally suited to the smaller tank or nano-reef. It is easy to feed, fairly disease-resistant and highly likable for its behaviors and character. (Despite its labelling by fishsellers, it is not a hawkfish, but a close relative.)

FEEDING: Carnivore. Feed at least once daily with meaty frozen and fresh foods, including mysid shrimp and enriched brine shrimp.

HABITAT: Reef. Its natural tendency is to lurk within rocky hiding places, resting at the entrance of a shelter, making brief forays into the open. Provide it with nooks, crannies and caves.

COMPATIBILITY: More than one of these likable little perchlets can be kept in a medium to large aquarium. However, males may fight (males are generally larger than females). House it with small, passive fish species (blennies, smaller cardinalfishes, small wrasses, dragonets, gobies, dartfishes). Its small size also makes it a potential meal for large fish eaters and a target of benthic bullies (e.g., dottybacks, hawkfishes). Larger specimens may eat nano-gobies and tiny shrimp, but it is generally safe with ornamental invertebrates.

AQUARIUM BEHAVIOR: The Unarmed Perchlet can be quite secretive, but will spend more time in the open with dither fish species, such as *Chromis* spp., flasher wrasses or forktail blennies. It is prone to jumping, especially from tanks without adequate shelter and hiding places.

YELLOW ASSESSOR *Assessor flavissimus*
(Yellow Devilfish)

MAXIMUM LENGTH: 2.2 in. (5.9 cm).

NATIVE RANGE: West Pacific.

MINIMUM AQUARIUM SIZE: 10 gal. (38 L).

OVERVIEW: This Great Barrier Reef species is very hardy, has a unique color pattern and lives in caves. It is an outstanding choice for the peaceful reef aquarium. The Blue Assessor (*Assessor macneilli*) is a similar species with identical traits and husbandry requirements.

FEEDING: Carnivore. Feed meaty foods at least once a day, perhaps less frequently in a well-established, productive reef system with ample live feeding opportunities.

HABITAT: Reef. An aquascape having one or more overhangs or large caves is best and will allow the aquarist to watch the assessor's natural behaviors.

COMPATIBILITY: This species occurs singly or in pairs or small groups in the wild, and solitary individuals do fine on their own in an aquarium. Although more than one can be kept in a larger system, in small tanks they will quarrel. If a pair or group is kept, acquire individuals of differing sizes. They are rarely aggressive toward other fishes, although they may dart at smaller fishes that invade their preferred hideouts. On the other hand, they are a likely target of more aggressive tankmates, especially the more belligerent dottybacks. The Yellow Assessor will not bother ornamental invertebrates.

AQUARIUM BEHAVIOR: Shy when first added to the tank, but will become quite bold in time. It will be seen swimming upside-down alone if a good cave or ledge is present in the tank.

BICOLOR BLENNY *Ecsenius bicolor*

MAXIMUM LENGTH: 4 in. (10 cm).

NATIVE RANGE: Indo-Pacific.

MINIMUM AQUARIUM SIZE: 20 gal. (76 L).

OVERVIEW: A comical little fish that has lots of character, this is an excellent, easy-to-keep community species that also has an interesting chromatic scheme with at least three different color phases.

FEEDING: Herbivore. Feed frozen and flake foods containing marine algae and spirulina at least once a day (if little algae is present in the tank, feed more often).

HABITAT: Reef. Provide plenty of hiding places, preferably small holes that it can back into. If necessary, use a ½- to-¾-inch drill bit to create some holes in the soft coral rock.

COMPATIBILITY: The Bicolor Blenny is rarely aggressive toward other fishes, with the exception of other blennies (especially others in the same genus). Aggression is usually not a problem in a tank of 75 gallons (285 L) or more. In very small tanks, it may chase passive zooplankton feeders like dartfishes and firefishes. Keep singly unless the tank is large. They will be more congenial to one another if you acquire a male and female (unfortunately there is no known way to distinguish sex by external characteristics). This fish is generally safe in a reef tank, but may nip at clam mantles and coral polyps.

AQUARIUM BEHAVIOR: The Bicolor Blenny will spend most of its time resting on the aquarium rockwork or nipping at the glass or hard substrate. When resting, it will back into small holes with only its head protruding or perch, in repose, on the live rock.

CANARY FANG BLENNY *Meiacanthus oualanensis*

MAXIMUM LENGTH: 4.3 in. (11 cm).

NATIVE RANGE: West Pacific.

MINIMUM AQUARIUM SIZE: 30 gal. (114 L).

OVERVIEW: This bright yellow blenny has both beauty and a secret weapon—venomous fangs. While not a risk for the aquarist or non-aggressive tankmates, it will bite in self-defense if another fish attempts to attack it.

FEEDING: Carnivore. Feed small meaty foods, including *Mysis* shrimp and frozen or dried cyclops, at least twice a day. It will graze on small invertebrates that live in live rock and may need to be fed more often if these animals are not present in your tank.

HABITAT: Reef. It needs small holes in which to hide.

COMPATIBILITY: This blenny will ignore its tankmates as long as they do not attempt to eat it, in which case any attacker is in store for an unexpected dose of pain. A large fish that swallows one of these blennies will usually be bitten in the mouth after ingesting its prey. Once introduced to this fish's large fangs, even aggressive tankmates will typically ignore them. Keep only one per tank (can be kept in heterosexual pairs, but they are difficult to sex). You can keep it with other members of the genus *Meiacanthus* (add all members of the genus to the tank simultaneously).

AQUARIUM BEHAVIOR: It is not afraid to spend much of its time hovering and swimming in the open. When it hides, it usually backs into holes with its head protruding. Captive spawning does occur.

MIDAS BLENNY *Ecsenius midas*

MAXIMUM LENGTH: 5.1 in. (13 cm).

NATIVE RANGE: Indo-Pacific.

MINIMUM AQUARIUM SIZE: 20 gal. (76 L).

OVERVIEW: A nonconformist among the blennies, this species spends much of its time feeding in the water column on zooplankton rather than staying close to the protection of the substrate. Its color can be stunning—matching that of the glorious Lyretail Anthias, with which it is often found swimming and feeding in the wild.

FEEDING: Omnivore. Feed a variety of foods, including both meaty and algae-containing foods, at least twice per day.

HABITAT: Reef. Provide plenty of hiding places, preferably small holes that it can back into. You can use a ½- to-¾-inch drill bit to create some of these in the rock.

COMPATIBILITY: The Midas Blenny will usually ignore its tankmates. On rare occasions, it may pick on smaller, passive species, especially in tight quarters. It is best to keep one per tank, unless your aquarium is large (100 gallons [380 L] or more), in which case you should be able to keep a pair. This species mostly plucks its food from open water and is less likely to pick at clams and corals.

AQUARIUM BEHAVIOR: This species divides its day swimming in the water column or peeking from a favorite burrow in the rockwork. It will dash about to snatch food as it floats past in the current. In a large aquarium, it would make an interesting tankmate for a shoal of Lyretail Anthias. It may leap from an open tank when startled.

SAILFIN BLENNY *Emblemaria diphyodontis*

MAXIMUM LENGTH: 2 in. (5 cm).

NATIVE RANGE: Tropical West Atlantic.

MINIMUM AQUARIUM SIZE: 10 gal. (38 L).

OVERVIEW: This comical, fascinating little fish is the perfect addition to the smaller tank. The large sail-like fin is raised in response to competing males or attractive females. In large community aquariums with competitive, boisterous tankmates, it is likely to hide constantly and not be able to get sufficient nourishment.

FEEDING: Carnivore. Feed meaty foods, at least once a day.

HABITAT: Reef. Provide plenty of rocks with small holes (e.g., hard tubeworm tubes) that they can back into.

COMPATIBILITY: This is a peaceful species that can be kept with many other small, passive fishes. Its small size makes it a potential snack to many fish-eating species (e.g., frogfishes, scorpionfishes, groupers, snappers); pick its neighbors very carefully. It may also be accosted by aggressive species like dottybacks and damselfishes. You can keep several, even in a smaller tank, as long as everyone has his or her own hole. It is a wonderful addition to the reef tank, although you may have difficulty finding it in a larger reef aquarium because of all the potential hiding holes.

AQUARIUM BEHAVIOR: The Sailfin Blenny and its kin spend most of their time with their heads peeking out of their "home" hole. They watch vigilantly for an appropriately sized food item to float past and then rapidly race out to pick it off.

TAILSPOT BLENNY *Ecsenius stigmatura*

MAXIMUM LENGTH: 2 in. (5 cm).

NATIVE RANGE: West Pacific.

MINIMUM AQUARIUM SIZE: 20 gal. (76 L).

OVERVIEW: This is a wonderful fish for a marine community tank. It exhibits an interesting color pattern, including orange and blue eye liners, and spends more time in open water swimming about than many other blennies.

FEEDING: Omnivore. Feed meaty as well as herbivore foods at least twice per day.

HABITAT: Reef. Provide plenty of hiding places, preferably small holes that it can back into. Use a ½- to-¾-inch drill bit to create some holes in the live rock.

COMPATIBILITY: This blenny is very neighborly. It rarely bothers tank-mates, including other smaller blennies. If it has been in a tank for a while, it will assert its dominance over newly introduced members of the same genus (especially in a smaller aquarium). It is likely to be picked on by dottybacks, more aggressive damselfishes, and hawk-fishes. You can keep more than one in a tank of 75 gallons (285 L) or larger. More than one individual can be housed in a larger tank. It seldom picks at clams or corals.

AQUARIUM BEHAVIOR: The Tailspot Blenny spends almost an equal amount of time resting in its favorite hiding hole and swimming about the aquarium looking for food. It does not appear to be a big algae eater, like others in the family. Keep in a covered tank.

AURIGA BUTTERFLYFISH *Chaetodon auriga*
(Threadfin Butterflyfish)

MAXIMUM LENGTH: 9.1 in. (23 cm).

NATIVE RANGE: Indo-Pacific.

MINIMUM AQUARIUM SIZE: 100 gal. (380 L).

OVERVIEW: Here is one of the best all-around butterflyfishes for the fish-only marine community aquarium. It is a handsome fish that exhibits many of the stereotypic behavioral and chromatic characteristics of its large and fascinating family. It differs in being much hardier than most other butterflyfish species. At full size, it will require a larger-than-average aquarium.

FEEDING: Carnivore. Feed a variety of meaty foods at least three times a day. Regular supplementation of its diet with color-enhancing foods will help maintain its beautiful pigmentation.

HABITAT: Reef or reef-sand interface. Provide plenty of swimming room for this fish.

COMPATIBILITY: The Auriga Butterflyfish is a good community fish, but will exhibit hostility toward members of its own kind and other butterflyfishes with similar color patterns. It tends to ignore unrelated species. Like most of the members of its family, this fish is not suitable for the reef aquarium, as it will feed on a wide variety of ornamental invertebrates.

AQUARIUM BEHAVIOR: The Auriga Butterflyfish will swim boldly about the tank, regularly stopping to inspect the aquascape for food. If you can acquire a female-male pair, they will swim in close proximity to each other and occasionally perform a "greeting display" upon reuniting after a short time of foraging apart.

DOUBLESADDLE BUTTERFLYFISH *Chaetodon ulietensis*
(Pacific Doublesaddle Butterflyfish, False Falcula Butterflyfish)

MAXIMUM LENGTH: 5.9 in. (15 cm).

NATIVE RANGE: Indo-Pacific.

MINIMUM AQUARIUM SIZE: 75 gal. (285 L).

OVERVIEW: Sporting classic yellow, white and black butterflyfish attire, this durable species is a welcome addition to the fish-only tank. It resembles the attractive Falcula Butterflyfish (*C. falcula*).

FEEDING: Omnivore. Feed a varied diet of meaty and algae-based foods, at least three times a day.

HABITAT: Reef or reef-sand interface. Provide plenty of swimming room for this fish.

COMPATIBILITY: Butterflyfishes are not generally aggressive, except with their own kind. It is prudent to keep only one Doublesaddle Butterflyfish per tank, unless you can acquire a known male-female pair. They will not only chase members of their own kind, but may also behave aggressively toward other species in the family that are similar in color. It feeds on a variety of invertebrates, including zoanthids, sea anemones, stony corals and soft-corals.

AQUARIUM BEHAVIOR: Like others in the family, it is an active fish that will spend most of its time in the open. If threatened, it will dash into a hole or crevice. They may be retiring when first introduced, but learn to recognize their keepers as a source of food and become bolder in time. Juveniles between 2 and 3.1 in. (5.1 and 7.9 cm) adjust most easily to aquarium life.

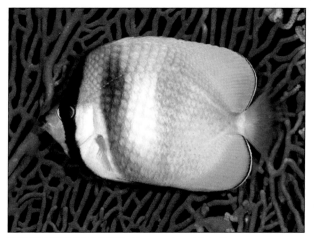

KLEIN'S BUTTERFLYFISH *Chaetodon kleinii*
(Brown Butterflyfish, Corallicola Butterflyfish)

MAXIMUM LENGTH: 5.5 in. (14 cm).

NATIVE RANGE: Indo-Pacific.

MINIMUM AQUARIUM SIZE: 55 gal. (209 L).

OVERVIEW: Although it may not be the most attractive member of the family, it is one of the most durable chaetodontids and a great choice for beginning or intermediate hobbyists.

HABITAT: Reef or reef-sand interface. Provide plenty of swimming room for this fish.

FEEDING: Omnivore. Feed a varied diet of meaty and algae-based foods at least three times a day. All butterflyfishes benefit from regular feedings of color-enhancing enriched foods.

COMPATIBILITY: It is possible to keep a pair of these fish in a larger aquarium. Males will fight—unfortunately, telling the differences between the sexes is difficult. Be prepared to separate individuals if they start quarreling frequently. It rarely bothers unrelated fishes, although it may fight with more aggressive butterflyfishes. Known bullies (large damselfishes, some angelfishes, surgeonfishes, triggerfishes) may pick on this fish. This species is not suitable for the reef aquarium, as it feeds heavily on soft corals in the wild and will happily eat a wide variety of ornamental invertebrates in the aquarium.

AQUARIUM BEHAVIOR: Klein's Butterflyfish swims just over the aquarium bottom when searching for grazing opportunities or into the water column to intercept suspended food.

LEMON BUTTERFLYFISH *Chaetodon miliaris*
(Milletseed Butterflyfish)

MAXIMUM LENGTH: 5.1 in. (13 cm).

NATIVE RANGE: Hawaiian Islands and Johnston Atoll.

MINIMUM AQUARIUM SIZE: 75 gal. (285 L).

OVERVIEW: The Lemon Butterflyfish is probably the hardiest of the American native butterflyfishes, making its home on the reefs of the Aloha State. It is a good choice as a first butterflyfish.

FEEDING: Omnivore. Feed a varied diet of meaty and algae-based foods at least three times a day. Yellow individuals may fade in color if not given color-enhancing foods at least several times each week.

HABITAT: Reef or reef-sand interface. Swimming space is important for this species.

COMPATIBILITY: This is a peaceful butterflyfish that can be kept in pairs or even in small groups if the tank is large enough. If one individual starts picking on others, remove the bully. It is not inclined to bother other fish tankmates, but may be badgered by the "usual suspects" (large damselfishes, some angelfishes, surgeonfishes, triggerfishes). This species is not suitable for most reef aquariums, as it will feed on a wide variety of ornamental invertebrates—but it is sometimes kept with unpalatable, tree-like soft corals.

AQUARIUM BEHAVIOR: In nature, the Lemon Butterflyfish spends lots of time swimming in the open water looking for zooplankton. In the aquarium, it spends time in both the water column and just above the aquarium substrate.

LONGFIN BANNERFISH *Heniochus acuminatus*
(Threadfin Bannerfish, Pennant Coralfish)

MAXIMUM LENGTH: 9.8 in. (25 cm).

NATIVE RANGE: Indo-West Pacific.

MINIMUM AQUARIUM SIZE: 100 gal. (380 L).

OVERVIEW: With dramatic markings and elegant finnage, this handsome fish will readily acclimate to the larger home aquarium. It is one of several butterflyfishes that will clean parasites from other fishes.

FEEDING: Omnivore. Feed a varied diet of meaty and algae-based foods at least three times a day.

HABITAT: Reef or reef-sand interface. Provide plenty of swimming room for this fish.

COMPATIBILITY: The Longfin Bannerfish can be kept in small schools in a larger home aquarium. It is prudent to add all members of the group simultaneously. Group members will form a pecking order. When battling for dominance, they will head-butt and attempt to push their opponents backward. This species is not a good addition to the reef tank, because it will pick on a wide range of ornamental invertebrates (including soft and stony corals). The similar-looking Schooling Bannerfish (*H. diphreutes*) is a dedicated planktivore and much less likely to eat corals.

AQUARIUM BEHAVIOR: This species will swim in the open in the home aquarium, although it will feel more secure and behave more naturally if it has several rocky hideouts available. Individuals may live as long as 19 years in captivity.

BUTTERFLYFISH I PEACEFUL

LONGNOSE BUTTERFLYFISH *Forcipiger flavissimus*
(Yellow Longnose Butterflyfish, Forceps Fish)

MAXIMUM LENGTH: 8.7 in. (22 cm).

NATIVE RANGE: Indo-Pacific.

MINIMUM AQUARIUM SIZE: 75 gal. (285 L).

OVERVIEW: With its extremely elongate beak or snout, this distinctive butterflyfish has a pair of needle-nose pliers for jaws, which it uses to amputate the tentacles of tube worms, and the tube feet and pedicellariae of sea urchins. It is a wonderful aquarium fish.

FEEDING: Carnivore. Feed a varied diet of meaty foods, such as mysid shrimp and protein-rich reef rations, twice a day.

HABITAT: Reef or reef-sand interface. Provide plenty of swimming room for this fish.

COMPATIBILITY: While this fish is typically a model aquarium resident in the fish-only aquarium, it has been known to occasionally pick on corals in the reef tank. It will also mutilate certain sessile invertebrates with its long jaws. It will fight with members of its own kind, so it is best to keep only one per tank. Although this species will consistently do better if kept in a peaceful community tank, it can be housed with moderately aggressive tankmates. It should be acclimated to the tank before the tougher competitors are introduced.

AQUARIUM BEHAVIOR: When harassed by other fishes, it will direct its long, stout dorsal spines toward the aggressor to defend itself. The similar Big Longnose Butterflyfish (*Forcipiger longirostris*) has a more elongate snout and is not quite as robust in captivity.

BANGGAI CARDINALFISH *Pterapogon kauderni*
(Banner Cardinalfish, Highfin Cardinalfish)

MAXIMUM LENGTH: 3 in. (7.6 cm).

NATIVE RANGE: Indonesia.

MINIMUM AQUARIUM SIZE: 30 gal. (114 L).

OVERVIEW: This remarkable fish has decorative finnage, a striking color pattern, and practices a very unique reproductive mode that enables the aquarist to more easily raise these fish in the home aquarium. It may also live in certain sea anemones in the aquarium.

FEEDING: Carnivore. Feed meaty foods at least twice a day.

HABITAT: Native to lagoons with sandy substrates and seagrasses. If you have the appropriate system, they can be housed with a Longspined Sea Urchin (*Diadema setosum*), which is used as shelter in the wild.

COMPATIBILITY: This species is rarely quarrelsome toward fish tank-mates. It may bicker with other cardinalfish in a smaller tank, but usually minds its own business. However, adults will fight with each other, sometimes to the death. If you add a group, two individuals will usually pair up and begin picking on others in the group. It rarely bothers invertebrates.

AQUARIUM BEHAVIOR: Try to select only captive-raised individuals, as wild-caught Banggai Cardinalfish have problems acclimating to the home aquarium. The male incubates the eggs in its mouth and also broods the young fish after they hatch. When they are finally expelled from the mouth, the fry will accept brine shrimp nauplii, both live and frozen.

PAJAMA CARDINALFISH *Sphaeramia nematoptera*

MAXIMUM LENGTH: 3.1 in. (7.9 cm).

NATIVE RANGE: West Pacific.

MINIMUM AQUARIUM SIZE: 20 gal. (76 L).

OVERVIEW: With bright-red eyes and a polka-dotted posterior, the Pajama Cardinalfish is a one-of-a-kind species that is almost "bullet-proof" and one of the very best species for the new marine aquarist.

FEEDING: Carnivore. Feed meaty foods, such as mysid shrimp and frozen or live adult brine shrimp, at least twice a day. Regular feeding with color-enhancing rations will help avoid loss of pigmentation.

HABITAT: Reef. Associates with branching *Porites* coral colonies in quiet bays. Will also use rocky crevices and caves for shelter.

COMPATIBILITY: This fish often does best when housed with members of its own kind. Group members will set up a pecking order, with the largest individual being the most dominant. Fortunately, aggressive exchanges within a social group usually consist of the occasional chase or nudge. If you are hoping to acquire a male and female, it has been reported that males have a longer filament on the second dorsal fin than females (this has not been confirmed by internal examination). They usually ignore other fish species, although they may exhibit some mild aggression toward other cardinalfishes.

AQUARIUM BEHAVIOR: The Pajama Cardinalfsih is a nocturnal species that may take refuge among branching corals or near a crevice during the day, becoming more active and foraging for food at night. It is very disease-resistant and may spawn in the home aquarium.

YELLOWSTRIPED CARDINALFISH *Apogon cyanosoma*
(Orangestriped Cardinalfish)

MAXIMUM LENGTH: 3.1 in. (7.9 cm).

NATIVE RANGE: Indo-West Pacific.

MINIMUM AQUARIUM SIZE: 20 gal. (76 L).

OVERVIEW: This is a commendably hardy and brightly colored cardinalfish that is regularly found in groups in the wild, hovering over or amid the tentacles of certain sea anemones or the spines of sea urchins.

FEEDING: Carnivore. Feed meaty foods, including enriched brine shrimp, mysid shrimp and squid at least twice a day.

HABITAT: Reef. Provide numerous hiding places. The invertebrates that often serve as wild hosts (sea anemones and sea urchins) can be more difficult to keep in captivity.

COMPATIBILITY: More than one Yellowstriped Cardinalfish can be housed together—this is a nice way to replicate their natural shoaling instincts. However, if crowded in too small a space, they may quarrel. To keep a small group, add all individuals (preferably an odd number) simultaneously to a larger tank with plenty of hiding places. This cardinalfish can be kept with a wide array of other fish species and invertebrates, although it may be tempted to dine on tiny, delicate ornamental targets, such as the anemone shrimps (*Periclimenes* spp.).

AQUARIUM BEHAVIOR: While many cardinalfishes are nocturnal, this species will spend its daylight hours at the entrance of a cave or crevice. It has been successfully bred in captivity.

CLARK'S CLOWNFISH *Amphiprion clarkii*
(Clark's Anemonefish, Yellowtail Clownfish)

MAXIMUM LENGTH: 5.5 in. (14 cm).
NATIVE RANGE: Indo-West Pacific.
MINIMUM AQUARIUM SIZE: 30 gal. (114 L).
OVERVIEW: Attractive and easy to feed and keep, this is one of the bigger, bolder clownfishes, also known as anemonefishes for their close association with sea anemones in the wild. It is often mislabeled as the Sebae Clownfish, a smaller, less-robust species.
FEEDING: Omnivore. Feed meaty and algae-based foods at least twice a day.
HABITAT: Reef, always in association with a sea anemone in the wild, but does not need a host to thrive in the aquarium.
COMPATIBILITY: This is a large, rough-mannered clownfish that does best with other pugnacious species (angelfishes, surgeonfishes, large wrasses). Smaller fishes may be attacked and injured—especially in smaller aquariums. They may also eat small shrimps or even feed them to their hosts. Keep only one per tank unless you can get them to pair up (add juveniles to the tank and one will usually become a functional female, while a less-dominant individual will develop male sex organs, and others, if any, act as passive standbys).
AQUARIUM BEHAVIOR: Clark's Clownfish will swim about the tank between episodes of diving among the tentacles of its anemone host if one is present. Anemones can be very difficult to keep. The ideal choice is a captive-propagated Bubbletip Anemone (*Entacmaea quadricolor*). Also select tank-raised clownfishes whenever possible.

MAROON CLOWNFISH *Premnas biaculeatus*
(Spinecheek Anemonefish)

MAXIMUM LENGTH: 6.3 in. (16 cm).

NATIVE RANGE: Indo-West Pacific.

MINIMUM AQUARIUM SIZE: 30 gal. (114 L).

OVERVIEW: This large and vividly colored clownfish is a hardy favorite of marine aquarists, but is too territorial to be housed in a smaller, peaceful community tank.

FEEDING: Omnivore. Feed meaty and algae-based foods at least twice a day. Color-enhancing rations can help maintain its bright colors.

HABITAT: Reef. In the wild, it almost always associates with the Bubbletip Anemone (*Entacmaea quadricolor*). While most captive individuals are finicky, some Maroon Clownfish will settle in with a variety of anemone species (including the Atlantic Pink-tipped Sea Anemone, *Condylactis gigantea*). It can be kept without a host.

COMPATIBILITY: This fish should be housed with relatively big, bold tankmates (angelfishes, surgeonfishes, bigger wrasses). While a female and male can be kept together, it can be difficult to keep females from "nagging" a male to death, especially in a smaller tank. The female pair member is often three or more times larger than her masculine partner. It will also harass other clownfish-fish and more passive fish tankmates.

AQUARIUM BEHAVIOR: This clownfish usually stays fairly close to its host. It will sally out into the water column to pick off floating food particles. Select captive-raised individuals whenever possible. A color morph with gold bands is sometimes available.

OCELLARIS CLOWNFISH *Amphiprion ocellaris*
(Common Anemonefish, False Percula Clownfish)

MAXIMUM LENGTH: 3.5 in. (8.9 cm).

NATIVE RANGE: Indo-West Pacific.

MINIMUM AQUARIUM SIZE: 10 gal. (38 L).

OVERVIEW: Well-known for its starring role in the movie "Finding Nemo," this endearing little fish is a welcome introduction to more peaceful community settings, small and large tanks alike.

FEEDING: Omnivore. Feed meaty and algae-based foods at least twice a day. Color-enhancing foods can help it maintain its bright colors.

HABITAT: In the wild, it is found with a host sea anemone (often *Heteractis magnifica*, the Magnificent Anemone—a species that is very hard to keep in captivity). However, this fish is easily kept and even bred without an anemone. It may adopt a surrogate host—a patch of hair algae, some coral polyps or even a feather duster worm.

COMPATIBILITY: This is one of the more passive clownfishes. Although it is best kept in pairs, if you purchase two juveniles, one will transform into a female, while a subordinate individual will become a male. They rarely bother other clownfish, but are often the target of more belligerent relatives. The Ocellaris Clownfish is also harmless toward non-related fishes and invertebrates, making it one of the best clownfishes for the community aquarium or nano-reef.

AQUARIUM BEHAVIOR: This gorgeous little fish seems to wriggle like a puppy when excited, undulating in a serpentine-like manner that never fails to amuse observers. Always seek out captive-raised individuals, as they acclimate more readily than wild-caught fish.

CLOWNFISH | PEACEFUL

TOMATO CLOWNFISH *Amphiprion frenatus*
(Tomato Anemonefish)

MAXIMUM LENGTH: 5.5 in. (14 cm).

NATIVE RANGE: Indo-West Pacific.

MINIMUM AQUARIUM SIZE: 30 gal. (114 L).

OVERVIEW: Sporting a red to reddish orange color scheme, this is a flashy and almost indestructible fish. Its durability is only matched by its potential pugnaciousness in smaller tanks.

FEEDING: Omnivore. Feed meaty and vegetable foods at least twice a day. Color-enhancing foods can help maintain its bright colors.

HABITAT: Reef. In nature, it lives in a sea anemone, but does not need a host to thrive in the aquarium. If an appropriate sea anemone is not present, it will find shelter in reef crevices or behind decor.

COMPATIBILITY: This gorgeous member of the clownfish guild may behave badly and be very territorial as an adult. While young fish may get along well with others (at least, unrelated species), adults may bite any fish that gets close to its host. Some individuals are less aggressive if a sea anemone is not present in the aquarium. Can be kept singly or in heterosexual pairs—the female is larger and usually darker in color than the male.

AQUARIUM BEHAVIOR: The preferred host of this species is the Bubbletip Anemone (*Entacmaea quadricolor*). It will swim in the water column, diving into a shelter when threatened. Tank-raised fish and anemones are the best choices. (Both are under heavy collection pressure in the wild, and captive-bred animals are the ethical choice and are much more likely to thrive in the aquarium.)

COMET *Calloplesiops altivelis*
(Marine Betta, Sea Betta)

MAXIMUM LENGTH: 7.9 in. (20 cm).

NATIVE RANGE: Indo-West Pacific.

MINIMUM AQUARIUM SIZE: 55 gal. (209 L).

OVERVIEW: This spotted beauty exhibits interesting hunting behaviors and is also one of the most durable fishes available to the home aquarist.

FEEDING: Carnivore. Feed meaty foods such as mysis shrimp, krill, carnivore rations or grated fresh or frozen seafood two or three times a week. Occasional meals of live foods, such as adult brine shrimp, will be eaten with relish.

HABITAT: Reef. Needs suitable caves and crevices to shelter in.

COMPATIBILITY: This fish will "slurp up" very small fishes (e.g., tiny gobies) and shrimp. When the Comet hunts, it tips its body forward, erects its huge pelvic fins and curls its tail to one side. It propels itself toward its potential victim by undulating the pectoral fins. This exaggerated approach may distract the Comet's victim, and the extended pelvic fins and tail form a barrier to impede the prey's escape. It seldom bothers its tankmates, except for members of its own kind, and is best kept singly. If a pair can be acquired, they may lay a gelatinous mass of eggs in a hole or crevice. The male guards the eggs.

AQUARIUM BEHAVIOR: This fish is very shy, spending much of its time hiding when first added to a tank. With time, it will make longer appearances in open areas, occasionally displaying its elegant form as it slowly moves from one hiding place to another. It will never be especially bold.

CONVICT BLENNY *Pholidichthys leucotaenia*
(Convict Worm Blenny)

MAXIMUM LENGTH: 13.4 in. (34 cm)

NATIVE RANGE: Indo-West Pacific

MINIMUM AQUARIUM SIZE: 30 gal. (114 L)

OVERVIEW: This is an oddity, a dramatically pigmented eel-like blenny that will mate and even produce young in the aquarium. However interesting, it loves to burrow under rock and can be very rough on an aquarium aquascape.

FEEDING: Carnivore. Feed meaty foods at least once a day.

HABITAT: Reef-sand interface. Be sure that the rockwork in the tank is stable and resting on the tank bottom (not on the sand), as this species may undermine the reef structure and cause it to collapse.

COMPATIBILITY: The juveniles can be kept in groups, but remember they grow quite large and can really tear up a tank. Adults are usually congenial to one another and often pair-up. Larger adults will eat small fishes and ornamental crustaceans.

AQUARIUM BEHAVIOR: This interesting fish lives in schools as a juvenile, mimicking venomous Coral Catfish (*Plotosus lineatus*) and spends its time milling about in the water column. As it grows, its stripes shift from longitudinal to vertical and it begins spending time on or near the bottom. They have been known to spawn in the home aquarium producing a benthic egg bundle and then brooding the young, which includes sucking them into their mouths and spitting them back into a favorite crevice. Spawning usually takes place in a cave or burrow and the first sign the aquarist may see is the emergence of the young blennies.

BLUE CHROMIS *Chromis cyanea*

MAXIMUM LENGTH: 5.1 in. (13 cm).

NATIVE RANGE: Tropical Western Atlantic, Caribbean.

MINIMUM AQUARIUM SIZE: 55 gal. (209 L).

OVERVIEW: With electric-blue scales and jet-black trim stripes, this is an active species that makes a flashy, welcome addition to both fish-only and reef aquariums.

FEEDING: Carnivore. Feed a variety of meaty and algae-based foods at least twice a day. Color-enhancing foods can help maintain its bright pigmentation.

HABITAT: Reef. Provide plenty of suitable hiding places as well as a wide expanse of open water swimming space.

COMPATIBILITY: It can be kept singly or in groups (juveniles are often more comfortable in the latter). If more than one is housed in the same tank, dominance hierarchies will develop among individuals (a fish's position in the pecking order is a function of its size). It is often best to keep six or more in a larger tank, because in smaller groups those individuals on the bottom of the pecking order may be harassed to death. While the Blue Chromis is relatively peace loving, it may pick on small zooplankton eaters (as always, this is a bigger problem in a smaller tank).

AQUARIUM BEHAVIOR: This fish spends much of its time cruising the water column hunting for plankton. When first introduced or when stressed, its color will be dull, but once acclimated, it typically adopts a pleasing blue-and-black chromatic attire.

BLUE DEVIL *Chrysiptera cyanea*
(Blue Damsel, Sapphire Devil, Orangetail Damselfish)

MAXIMUM LENGTH: 3.1 in. (7.9 cm).
NATIVE RANGE: West Pacific.
MINIMUM AQUARIUM SIZE: 30 gal. (114 L).
OVERVIEW: A perennial favorite with neophyte fishkeepers, this glowing little species can have a big attitude, chastising smaller, less aggressive tankmates. Otherwise, it is a perfect aquarium inhabitant.
FEEDING: Omnivore. Feed meaty and algae-based foods at least once a day. Color-enhancing foods can help maintain its bright pigments.
HABITAT: Reef and rubble areas. The more hiding places the better to diffuse potential aggression.
COMPATIBILITY: This fish is best kept with more aggressive fishes and allowed to fend for itself. Housing it with more passive fishes is inviting trouble—especially if it is the first fish in the tank or the aquarium is small. You can keep more than one individual per tank—it is best to keep one male and one or more female (females have clear tails, the male's tail is blue or orange, depending on where the fish was collected). Larger males are most belligerent. It is not a threat to ornamental invertebrates.
AQUARIUM BEHAVIOR: The Blue Devil will dart and dash among aquarium decor, nipping substrate as it feeds on algae and tiny invertebrates. Safe with corals and clams. It may spawn in the home aquarium, laying eggs in a nest on a hard substrate. The male fans and guards the eggs until they hatch.

BLUEGREEN CHROMIS *Chromis viridis*
(Green Chromis, Bluegreen Damselfish)

MAXIMUM LENGTH: 3.9 in. (10 cm).
NATIVE RANGE: Indo-West Pacific.
MINIMUM AQUARIUM SIZE: 30 gal. (114 L).
OVERVIEW: With luminescent, shimmering colors when well fed, and under good lighting, a shoal of these attractive, unaggressive fishes can add color and movement to the reef or fish-only tank.
FEEDING: Omnivore. Feed a variety of meaty and algae-based foods at least twice a day. Color-enhancing foods can help it maintain its bright colors.
HABITAT: Shallow reef and lagoon areas above branching stony corals. Provide plenty of suitable hiding places.
COMPATIBILITY: Unlike many damselfishes, this species can—and should—be housed in groups. It is usually not a threat to unrelated tankmates, but group members will form a pecking order, with subordinates often receiving an unequal share of mistreatment from their kin. If the chromis group is large enough (six individuals or more), the aggression will be spread out so that no one subordinate gets too much abuse. It is not a threat to invertebrates and may help corals by swimming among their branches, encouraging circulation within the coral colony.
AQUARIUM BEHAVIOR: This species will spend most of its time racing around in the upper areas of the aquarium. They provide the look of an authentic reef and can act as "dither fishes," giving confidence to shy community members.

DOMINO DAMSEL *Dascyllus trimaculatus*
(Threespot Dascyllus)

MAXIMUM LENGTH: 5.5 in. (14 cm).

NATIVE RANGE: Indo-Pacific.

MINIMUM AQUARIUM SIZE: 55 gal. (209 L).

OVERVIEW: This fish is like a Doberman puppy—cute and cuddly when young, but potentially fearsome as an adult. They are indeed attractively marked and very durable, but often become unmanageable when they reach full size

FEEDING: Omnivore. Feed meaty and vegetable foods two or more times a day.

HABITAT: Reef. Provide plenty of hiding places—prefers stony coral colonies, juveniles will also live in sea anemones.

COMPATIBILITY: Many aquarists are attracted to the perky little juveniles, but they can become very aggressive toward each other and other fishes as they grow. While juveniles can be kept with a wide range of tankmates, adolescents and adults will pick on small, more passive fish tankmates. It is not unusual for young fish to pair up as they reach sexual maturity (other Domino Damsels will be harassed by the "happy couple").

AQUARIUM BEHAVIOR: The juveniles make a very attractive display as they bob up and down above a coral head or other shelter. As they get larger, they spend more time in the water column. This is a fish that survives conditions that wipe out other species, and it can live for over 20 years in captivity. It may also spawn in the aquarium.

GOLDBELLY DAMSEL *Pomacentrus auriventris*

MAXIMUM LENGTH: 2.8 in. (7.1 cm).

NATIVE RANGE: Indo-West Pacific.

MINIMUM AQUARIUM SIZE: 20 gal. (76 L).

OVERVIEW: A truly eyecatching beauty with deep-blue and bright-yellow chromatic highlights, this species readily settles into most home aquariums and has a more subdued temper than many other damselfishes.

FEEDING: Omnivore. Feed meaty and algae-based foods at least once a day. Regular offerings of color-enhancing foods can help maintain its intense pigmentation.

HABITAT: Reef, rubble areas and with macroalgae. Hiding places are essential to give this small species a sense of security.

COMPATIBILITY: This damselfish can be kept with less aggressive species if the tank is larger and it is added to the tank after its more sociable neighbors are settled. In a smaller aquarium, it may pick on newly introduced fishes. More than one Goldbelly can be housed in the same tank, but aggression within the group is less likely if the tank is larger and hiding places are plentiful. Adding a group of younger fish simultaneously also decreases the likelihood of conflict. They are not a threat to ornamental invertebrates and are a great choice for tanks with corals, giant clams and other reef creatures.

AQUARIUM BEHAVIOR: The Goldbelly Damsel adds color and interest to any aquarium, spending most of its time sculling just above the substrate or peering from a preferred hideout.

HUMBUG DASCYLLUS *Dascyllus aruanus*
(Fourstriped Damsel, Black and White Damsel)

MAXIMUM LENGTH: 3.1 in. (7.9 cm).

NATIVE RANGE: Indo-Pacific.

MINIMUM AQUARIUM SIZE: 30 gal. (114 L).

OVERVIEW: A dramatic, disruptive color pattern, as well as a strong constitution, has made this bold damselfish a favorite in new tanks and a good beginner's fish.

FEEDING: Omnivore. Feed meaty and algae-based foods at least once a day.

HABITAT: Reef. In nature, it lives in and near branching stony corals and is most comfortable when given plenty of sheltering places.

COMPATIBILITY: While youngsters make good neighbors, as they get larger, they can often become combative. Placing them in a small tank with smaller, passive species is asking for future troubles. In the wild, these fish live in stable groups consisting of three to 25 individuals. Attempting to replicate this natural social order can be difficult in captivity. Ideally, start with a group of juveniles and allow them to establish a pecking order. The most dominant fish will mature into a male (the subordinates will become females or be asexual). In a small tank, chaos may rule the day and only the most dominant fish will remain. They are good with ornamental invertebrates and will help oxygenate stony coral colonies.

AQUARIUM BEHAVIOR: This fish will usually hover near a staghorn-type coral colony, real or faux, waiting for food morsels to be swept past by water currents. It may spawn in the home aquarium.

TALBOT'S DEMOISELLE *Chrysiptera talboti*
(Talbot's Damsel)

MAXIMUM LENGTH: 2.4 in. (6.1 cm).

NATIVE RANGE: Indo-West Pacific.

MINIMUM AQUARIUM SIZE: 10 gal. (38 L).

OVERVIEW: This lesser-known yellow-hued demoiselle is as attractive and sturdy as others in the genus, but is less aggressive than most of its kin.

FEEDING: Omnivore. Feed meaty and vegetable foods at least once a day. Color-enhancing foods can help maintain its bright colors.

HABITAT: Reef. The more hiding places the better for this species. Abundant shelter enables this little fish to hide from potential threats and feel more secure.

COMPATIBILITY: Talbot's Demoiselle is not a threat to most tankmates, as it tends to have a congenial disposition. It rarely bothers non-related tankmates and is more likely to be the recipient of aggression. More than one can be housed per tank. To increase the likelihood of success, add only small individuals, or one large fish and one or more smaller *C. talboti*. Bickering between group members is more likely to become a problem in a smaller tank. This is a wonderful choice for the reef aquarium.

AQUARIUM BEHAVIOR: When it is not dashing about the tank, this demoiselle hovers over the substrate looking for passing food particles. The black spot at the base of its dorsal fin is known as an ocellus or false eye, and aids in confusing predators—their attacks are drawn away from the target's head and real eyes and are instead directed at the ocellus.

YELLOWTAIL DAMSEL *Chrysiptera parasema*
(Yellowtail Blue Damsel, Goldtail Demoiselle)

MAXIMUM LENGTH: 2.8 in. (7.1 cm).

NATIVE RANGE: West Pacific.

MINIMUM AQUARIUM SIZE: 10 gal. (38 L).

OVERVIEW: A marine aquarium classic, this is a wonderful species that is durable, colorful and not a bully.

FEEDING: Omnivore. Feed meaty and algae-based foods at least once a day. Color-enhancing foods can help it maintain its bright colors.

HABITAT: Reef, over and within thickets of branching *Acropora* corals. Provide with numerous sheltering hideouts.

COMPATIBILITY: The Yellowtail Damsel can be kept with less aggressive species, but it is best to add this damselfish to the tank last. In smaller quarters, it has been known to pester smaller fishes and is not a good choice for a nano-reef with any shy or passive tankmates. A small group can be kept in the same tank—males may quarrel, so add several smaller individuals and a single larger specimen (the males tend to be larger than the females). This species poses no threat to ornamental invertebrates and is an excellent choice for the reef aquarium.

AQUARIUM BEHAVIOR: The Yellowtail Damsel is primarily a zooplankton feeder that spends much of its time swimming just above the aquarium bottom looking for food. It will readily spawn in the home aquarium, although raising the larval young requires expert care and feeding.

SCISSORTAIL DARTFISH *Ptereleotris evides*
(Blackfin Dartfish, Scissortail Goby)

MAXIMUM LENGTH: 5.5 in. (14 cm).

NATIVE RANGE: Indo-Pacific.

MINIMUM AQUARIUM SIZE: 20 gal. (76 L).

OVERVIEW: Here is an unusual and likable addition to the peaceful community tank that will spend its time hovering in the open and darting about the aquarium. It is a good candidate to be kept in a small school.

FEEDING: Carnivore. Feed meaty foods, such as mysid shrimp and enriched adult brine shrimp, at least twice a day.

HABITAT: Reef-sand interface, lagoons and bays. Flat rocks with depressions dug underneath them provide excellent shelter sites.

COMPATIBILITY: This fish is very amiable and rarely, if ever, bothers other fish species. It may occasionaly display toward and briefly chase other dartfishes, but rarely harms them. If picked on by large or aggressively competitive tankmates, it will hide incessantly, will not eat, and will eventually perish. More than one can and should be housed in the same tank, as they tend to do better when in groups. It will not harm ornamental invertebrates.

AQUARIUM BEHAVIOR: When first added to the tank, the Scissortail Dartfish invariably goes into hiding. As it becomes comfortable with its new surroundings, it will begin swimming about in the water column. It is a proficient jumper that readily leaps from open aquariums. The tank must absolutely be kept tightly covered at all times.

ZEBRA DARTFISH *Ptereleotris zebra*
(Bar Goby, Chinese Zebra Goby)

MAXIMUM LENGTH: 4.3 in. (11 cm).

NATIVE RANGE: Indo-West Pacific and Red Sea.

MINIMUM AQUARIUM SIZE: 20 gal. (76 L).

OVERVIEW: An amiable, lovely fish that is not only beautiful and disease-resistant, but also engages in fascinating social behaviors when kept in groups.

FEEDING: Carnivore. Feed meaty plankton-like foods, such as mysid and enriched brine shrimp, at least twice a day.

HABITAT: Reef-sand interface. Flat rocks with depressions dug underneath them provide excellent shelter sites.

COMPATIBILITY: This is a happy-go-lucky species that gets along well with all of its tankmates, as long is they are not too large or belligerent. It also gets along well with its own kind and should be kept in pairs or small groups—they tend to acclimate more quickly and are more brazen when housed together. If harassed by more aggressive tankmates, this species will spend most of its time hiding and may eventually starve. It is an ideal species for a reef aquarium and not a threat to any ornamental invertebrates.

AQUARIUM BEHAVIOR: While shy when first added to the tank, this becomes a showy species, swimming about the water column, displaying at each other, and exhibiting typical zooplanktivore feeding behaviors. True to its name, it will dive into a hiding place when threatened. It is a proficient jumper—always keep the tank covered.

CARPET EEL BLENNY *Congrogadus subducens*
(Wolf Eel)

MAXIMUM LENGTH: 17.7 in. (45 cm).

NATIVE RANGE: Indo-West Pacific.

MINIMUM AQUARIUM SIZE: 20 gal. (76 L).

OVERVIEW: These odd-looking creatures actually belong to the dottyback family—they are neither eels nor blennies. The Carpet Eel Blenny can be brown or green overall, with varying degrees of lighter mottling and blotches. It acclimates easily to aquarium life.

FEEDING: Carnivore. Feed to satiation (or at least several large food items) two or three times per week. Feed frozen or fresh seafood. Live food may be required to get some to feed initially.

HABITAT: Reef. This fish spends most of its time squirming into interstices among rubble, or among rocks and benthic debris. It should be housed in a tank with numerous hiding places.

COMPATIBILITY: The Carpet Eel Blenny is a voracious predator that will eat small fishes and ornamental crustaceans. It will do best with larger fishes like squirrelfishes, soldierfishes, angelfishes, butterflyfishes, surgeonfishes and rabbitfishes. It can also be kept with more placid morays, although larger species will eat *C. subducens*. It is prudent to keep only one per tank, unless you can acquire a known heterosexual pair. When behaving aggressively toward a threat, they will open their jaws and flare their gill covers.

AQUARIUM BEHAVIOR: It will spend much of the time with its head sticking out of a crevice. The tank should have a secure top, as it is prone to leaping from open aquariums.

DIADEM DOTTYBACK *Pictichromis diadema*
(Diadem Basslet)

MAXIMUM LENGTH: 2.4 in. (6 cm).

NATIVE RANGE: West Pacific.

MINIMUM AQUARIUM SIZE: 10 gal. (38 L).

OVERVIEW: Part of a family as much known for its beauty as its assertiveness, this dottyback can be a brilliant addition to the right aquarium—a large tank or a small system with other pugnacious species. It has a notorious nasty streak, however, and can wreak havoc on a peaceful community tank.

FEEDING: Carnivore. Feed meaty foods, at least once a day. The magenta stripe along the back is prone to fading if you do not regularly provide the fish with color-enhancing rations.

HABITAT: Sheltered reefs. Lots of nooks and crannies are necessary for this species to acclimate.

COMPATIBILITY: Can be aggressive, especially in tight quarters. Keep one per tank unless the aquarium is very large. It is most likely to pick on other small species that live on or near the aquarium bottom (gobies, firefishes, small clownfishes). Feeds on small crustaceans and worms and so is not a threat to most ornamental invertebrates, although it may bother smaller shrimps.

AQUARIUM BEHAVIOR: In all ways typical of its family, the Diadem Dottyback can be fascinating to watch as it dashes from one crevice to another, occasionally stopping to scan the substrate or water column for food items. It is a survivor, but may take its toll on less aggressive species.

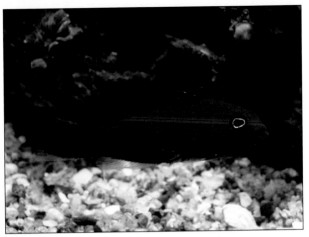

MAGENTA DOTTYBACK *Pictichromis porphyrea*
(Purple Dottyback, Strawberry Dottyback, Strawberry Basslet)

MAXIMUM LENGTH: 2.4 in. (6 cm).

NATIVE RANGE: West Pacific.

MINIMUM AQUARIUM SIZE: 10 gal. (38 L).

OVERVIEW: This magenta beauty will fluoresce as it flits about its aquarium home, but it has a feisty disposition and may bully smaller, more peaceful species.

FEEDING: Carnivore. Feed meaty foods, at least once per day. Its color may fade in the home aquarium, unless you provide a varied diet that includes color-enhancing pigments.

HABITAT: Outer reef slopes and walls. Provide numerous rocky hiding places with caves and crevices.

COMPATIBILITY: This is a potentially aggressive fish, especially in a smaller tank. If you want to keep it with other small fishes, it will need to be in a large tank (75 gal. [285 L] or more), replete with hiding places. A well-aquascaped reef aquarium is a perfect home. Keep one per tank. It will typically ignore ornamental invertebrates, with the possible exception of tiny shrimps (e.g., anemone shrimp). If pestered by more aggressive tankmates, it may hide incessantly and not get enough to eat.

AQUARIUM BEHAVIOR: This is a nervous little fish that relies on its speed and hiding places to avoid being eaten by predators. It will dash about the tank and occasionally stop to examine its world. It is sometimes confused with the Orchid Dottyback (*P. fridmani*), which has a distinctive black bar from its snout through its eye.

NEON DOTTYBACK *Pseudochromis aldabraensis*
(Aldabra Dottyback, Dutoiti Dottyback, Orange Dottyback)

MAXIMUM LENGTH: 3.3 in. (8 cm).

NATIVE RANGE: Indian Ocean, Arabian Gulf east to Pakistan.

MINIMUM AQUARIUM SIZE: 20 gal. (76 L).

OVERVIEW: With electric-blue bars on a bright-orange body, this is a flamboyantly colored species with fascinating, slinky moves, but one that can be a hellion in the wrong aquarium venue.

FEEDING: Carnivore. Feed meaty foods at least once a day. It is not as prone to color loss as some of its fellow dottybacks.

HABITAT: Reef. Provide numerous hiding places to help it acclimate more quickly and curb some of its aggressive tendencies.

COMPATIBILITY: The Neon Dottyback is almost guaranteed to cause behavior problems in a smaller tank. Keep singly. It will pick on and even kill smaller fishes, especially those that live on or near the substrate. It is best housed with fish tankmates having similar tough dispositions (pygmy angels, hawkfishes, large damselfishes, surgeonfishes), or in a very large reef aquarium where space and numerous hiding places will diffuse the aggressive behavior. It may attack ornamental shrimps.

AQUARIUM BEHAVIOR: The Neon Dottyback has a cryptic nature and will slither or dash from one crevice to another. It will often be observed hovering at the entrance of a refuge, scanning its environment. Most individuals now offered to aquarists are captive-raised and will spawn in the home aquarium.

ORCHID DOTTYBACK *Pseudochromis fridmani*
(Orchid Basslet)

MAXIMUM LENGTH: 2.8 in. (7 cm).

NATIVE RANGE: Red Sea.

MINIMUM AQUARIUM SIZE: 10 gal. (38 L).

OVERVIEW: Once a rarity that commanded breathtaking prices from well-heeled aquarists, this is a wonderful little reef fish that is both flashy and very hardy. Now being commercially bred in captivity, it has become affordable and widely available.

FEEDING: Carnivore. Feed meaty foods, at least once a day. Offer color-enhancing foods to prevent pigment loss, although it tends to be more colorfast than many others in the family.

HABITAT: Reef, in caves, under ledges and on vertical faces. Provide lots of holes and crevices for it to refuge in.

COMPATIBILITY: Although this species does not tend to be as aggressive as some in the family, it can bully more diminutive fishes, especially in smaller tanks where it will stake out its territory. Keep one per tank unless housed in a large aquarium or you can obtain a heterosexual pair. This is a great reef aquarium fish that typically ignores ornamental invertebrates, with the possible exception of delicate anemone shrimps or small fanworms.

AQUARIUM BEHAVIOR: The Orchid Dottyback will glide in the open water for brief periods and then disappear in a crevice. It often hangs at the entrance of its refuge to watch the world and wait for passing plankton. It is a fish that offers countless hours of watching pleasure.

SPRINGER'S DOTTYBACK *Pseudochromis springeri*
(Bluestriped Dottyback)

MAXIMUM LENGTH: 1.6 in. (4 cm).

NATIVE RANGE: Red Sea.

MINIMUM AQUARIUM SIZE: 10 gal. (38 L).

OVERVIEW: Jet black with bright blue blazing, this is an unusually beautiful and interesting-to-observe species. It is very durable and captive-raised individuals are readily available.

FEEDING: Carnivore. Feed meaty foods at least once a day. Color-enhancing foods will help prevent fading, although it tends to be more color-fast than many others in the family.

HABITAT: Reef. It will live among the branches of stony corals (live or skeletons) and in nooks and crannies in the live rock.

COMPATIBILITY: Like other dottybacks, Springer's Dottyback can present problems in a small tank, as it is prone to picking on smaller, substrate-oriented fishes such as gobies, dartfishes and blennies. Aggression is less problematic in a larger tank. Keep one per tank unless you can obtain a pair (try adding two smaller individuals, or one large and one small, to increase the likelihood of getting a male and female). It may bother small shrimps, but is otherwise not a threat to ornamental invertebrates.

AQUARIUM BEHAVIOR: This is a somewhat furtive fish that will dash about the tank, never very far from shelter, occasionally stopping at the opening of a hideout to assess its situation or to dash out to grab passing food items.

SUNRISE DOTTYBACK *Pseudochromis flavivertex*
(Flavivertex Basslet)

MAXIMUM LENGTH: 3.1 in. (8 cm).

NATIVE RANGE: Western Indian Ocean, Red Sea and Gulf of Aden.

MINIMUM AQUARIUM SIZE: 10 gal. (38 L).

OVERVIEW: Sporting a beautiful blue coloration with yellow flashes and yellow-rimmed eyes, this is an attractive and durable species that is less belligerent than many other dottybacks.

FEEDING: Carnivore. Feed meaty foods such as squid, mysid shrimp, and enriched brine shrimp at least once a day. Offer color-enhancing foods regularly to prevent fading of pigmentation.

HABITAT: Reef or reef-sand interface, often near coral heads. Provide numerous hiding places in a rocky aquascape.

COMPATIBILITY: Although not as aggressive as some of its kin, the Sunrise Dottyback can be a bully in a small tank, especially when housed with smaller, placid fishes. To keep this fish with peaceful species, house in a large tank loaded with live rock and plenty of sheltering places. It is most likely picked on by larger dottybacks, stocky hawkfishes, and large damselsfishes, especially in more confined quarters. Large individuals may attack ornamental shrimps.

AQUARIUM BEHAVIOR: This is a flighty little fish that will dart into a crevice when it detects a threat. It will become more brazen and spend more time in the open as it becomes accustomed to its aquarium home. Captive-bred specimens are now available and are highly recommended for their ability to acclimate to most home aquariums.

FANTAIL FILEFISH *Pervagor spilosoma*

MAXIMUM LENGTH: 7.1 in. (18 cm).

NATIVE RANGE: Hawaiian Islands.

MINIMUM AQUARIUM SIZE: 55 gal. (209 L).

OVERVIEW: Attractively spotted and unusual, this species has a large tail that spreads wide when displaying toward a rival or mate, and a large dorsal spine that it uses to wedge itself into hiding places.

FEEDING: Omnivore. Feed this fish meaty items, such as shrimp, squid and krill, as well as algae-based foods, three times per day.

HABITAT: Reef. Provide plenty of suitable hiding places.

COMPATIBILITY: The Fantail Filefish is not a very aggressive species, usually choosing to ignore its tankmates. However, there are some exceptions: this fish may squabble with other filefishes and with the related triggerfishes. It may also nip at sedentary species or bite at the elaborate fins of those fishes with long, flowing finnage. Keep one per tank unless you can acquire a mated pair. It brings a taste for corals and small invertebrates from the wild, and in the aquarium is a threat to coral polyps and a wide range of invertebrates. It is therefore best avoided by reefkeepers, although it will usually avoid sea anemones with potent stinging abilities.

AQUARIUM BEHAVIOR: While relatively shy when first added to a tank, the Fantail Filefish becomes quite bold in time. It will actively cruise the aquascape, following the rocky structure, pitching its body forward as it scans the bottom for food items. It will also take food from the water column. The filefishes are related to the pufferfishes, with which they share anatomical similarities.

FIREFISH *Nemateleotris magnifica*
(Red Firefish, Fire Dartfish, Magnificent Dartfish, Fire Goby)

Maximum Length: 3.1 in. (7.9 cm).

Native Range: Indo-Pacific.

Minimum Aquarium Size: 10 gal. (38 L).

Overview: Although timid in the presence of large and aggressive tankmates, this is a durable, attractive fish that can be kept in smaller aquariums and is perfect for the peaceful reef tank.

Feeding: Carnivore. Feed meaty foods, such as enriched brine shrimp and mysid shrimp, at least once a day.

Habitat: Reef-sand interface. Flat rocks with depressions dug underneath them provide excellent shelter sites.

Compatibility: While passive toward most other species, it will quarrel with members of its own kind. Therefore, it is best to keep one or a pair in the same tank. (The firefishes are often found as monogamous pairs in the wild.) Sexing individuals is difficult. Firefish have also been known to fight with their close relative, the Purple Firefish (*Nemateleotris decora*). These fish are potential prey for a wide variety of fish tankmates, so select their neighbors carefully. In a boisterous aquarium, it may hide constantly and not compete successfully for food. It is not a threat to ornamental invertebrates.

Aquarium Behavior: This lovely species hovers over the substrate, twitching its dorsal spine, possibly to communicate with members of its own kind. It takes most of its food from the water column. Firefishes are skilled jumpers; keep only in a covered aquarium.

PURPLE FIREFISH *Nemateleotris decora*
(Decorated Firefish, Elegant Firefish, Purple Dartfish, Flame Firefish)

MAXIMUM LENGTH: 3.5 in. (8.9 cm).

NATIVE RANGE: Indo-Pacific.

MINIMUM AQUARIUM SIZE: 10 gal. (38 L).

OVERVIEW: A truly alluring small fish, this is a beautiful, disease-resistant species that makes a wonderful addition to a reef tank or peaceful fish-only marine community aquarium. A similar species, Helfrich's Firefish (*Nemateleotris helfrichi*), is equally admirable, but much less common and usually priced as a rare fish.

FEEDING: Carnivore. Feed meaty plankton-like foods, such as mysid shrimp and enriched brine shrimp, at least once a day.

HABITAT: Reef-sand interface. Flat rocks with shallow caves or depressions dug underneath them provide excellent shelter sites.

COMPATIBILITY: This species will not behave aggressively toward other fishes, unless they are close relatives (primarily other firefish species). While they can be kept in pairs if you can acquire a male and female, males will fight with each other. They are not a threat to ornamental invertebrates and are an excellent choice for a peaceful reef aquarium.

AQUARIUM BEHAVIOR: This is a hovering species that hangs in the water column near a hiding place. If a threat arises, it will instantly dart into its burrow or hole. This species is one of the worst for making unintentional suicidal leaps from open aquariums. Be sure your tank is always properly covered.

BLACKRAY SHRIMP GOBY *Stonogobiops nematodes*
(Highfin Shrimp Goby, Filament-finned Prawn Goby, Antenna Goby)

MAXIMUM LENGTH: 2 in. (5.1 cm).

NATIVE RANGE: Indo-West Pacific.

MINIMUM AQUARIUM SIZE: 10 gal. (38 L).

OVERVIEW: This is one of many gobies that forms a symbiotic partnership with a snapping shrimp (*Alpheus* sp.), and this relationship can be amazing to watch in the home aquarium. This handsome shrimp goby species will readily adapt to a peaceful community tank. Try to acquire both fish and its crustacean partner, which will dig a burrow that they share for protection.

FEEDING: Carnivore. Feed meaty fresh and frozen foods—which will be eaten by both fish and shrimp—at least once a day.

HABITAT: Reef-sand interface. Provide some burrows or holes near the aquarium bottom where this fish can hide if not kept with its partner shrimp.

COMPATIBILITY: This is a peace-loving goby that will not bother other fish species. You can keep more than one in the same tank, but be sure they have enough space to spread out, and that there are appropriate hiding places and/or shrimp for each individual. Its small size and passive disposition means it is often the target of more pugnacious species. It is not a threat to ornamental invertebrates.

AQUARIUM BEHAVIOR: This shrimp goby spends more time hovering just over the substrate than most others in this guild. It often partners with the Tiger Snapping Shrimp (*Alpheus bellulus*) or Randall's Snapping Shrimp (*A. randalli*). Keep in a covered tank.

NEON GOBY *Elacatinus oceanops*

MAXIMUM LENGTH: 2 in. (5.1 cm).

NATIVE RANGE: Tropical Western Atlantic, Gulf of Mexico.

MINIMUM AQUARIUM SIZE: 10 gal. (38 L).

OVERVIEW: This streamlined, blue-streaked beauty cleans other fishes of ectoparasites, but readily accepts prepared aquarium foods. While the cleaning behaviors can be fascinating to watch, do not expect them to solve all disease problems you might encounter in the aquarium.

FEEDING: Carnivore. Feed meaty foods, such as Cyclop-Eeze, mysid shrimp and enriched brine shrimp, at least once a day.

HABITAT: Reef. Provide with overhangs, caves and crevices.

COMPATIBILITY: This lovely little fish is peace-loving and will only show hostility toward its close relatives. If the tank is large enough, these little fish will simply spread out over the captive reef rather than fight. They can also be kept in pairs in smaller tanks. The Neon Goby is not usually harassed by other fishes, although some of the more bellicose fishes may chase it, and some predatory species may attempt to eat it. It is not a threat to ornamental invertebrates.

AQUARIUM BEHAVIOR: The Neon Goby is a bottom-lover that will perch on mound-shaped corals or live rock. If a fish visits these spots and invites cleaning, it will oblige. It has been known to dart into the mouths of larger predators and remove parasites and bits of food from between their teeth. It regularly spawns in the home aquarium, laying benthic eggs in a hole. Raising the fry requires special care and feeding.

GOBY | PEACEFUL

PINKSPOTTED SHRIMP GOBY *Cryptocentrus leptocephalus* (Singapore Shrimp Goby, Pinkspotted Watchman Goby, Pinkspeckled Prawn Goby)

Maximum Length: 5.9 in. (15 cm).

Native Range: Indo-West Pacific.

Minimum Aquarium Size: 20 gal. (76 L).

Overview: This stunning shrimp goby is a fascinating addition to the home aquarium, especially if you can acquire its shrimp partner as well. The goby and shrimp are reported by some observers to team up for life, and it is always a shame to see them separated. A lone shrimp goby can be housed with an alpheid shrimp species, such as the common Tiger Snapping Shrimp (*Alpheus bellulus*), they may form a bond and share a burrow.

Feeding: Carnivore. Feed meaty fresh and frozen foods—which will be eaten by both fish and shrimp—at least once a day.

Habitat: Reef-sand interface. Provide some burrows or holes near the aquarium bottom where this fish can hide if you do not keep it with its burrowing partner shrimp.

Compatibility: This is a larger shrimp goby that may occasionally exhibit aggression toward others of its ilk, as well as small, passive fish species. That said, it is not overly belligerent. It has been known to eat ornamental shrimps, but is not a threat to other invertebrates.

Aquarium Behavior: This fish typically rests on the bottom, with its head protruding from a burrow or cave on the floor of the aquarium. It will swim into the water column to feed on floating food particles. It is an able jumper, so keep a top on its tank.

REDBANDED SHRIMP GOBY *Amblyeleotris fasciata*
(Redbanded Prawn Goby)

MAXIMUM LENGTH: 3.1 in. (7.9 cm).
NATIVE RANGE: West Pacific.
MINIMUM AQUARIUM SIZE: 10 gal. (38 L).
OVERVIEW: This is one of many gobies that forms a partnership with a snapping shrimp—a mutually beneficial symbiotic relationship that can be amazing to watch in the home aquarium.
FEEDING: Carnivore. Feed meaty foods at least once a day.
HABITAT: Reef-sand interface, with a deep sand bed. It will usually reside in a burrow that its partner shrimp digs under rocks. If a shrimp is not present, it will hide in rock crevices near the tank bottom.
COMPATIBILITY: This fish usually ignores its tankmates. Other small, benthic fish may be greeted with an open-mouth display if they try to invade its home, but otherwise, it is typically indifferent. It may quarrel with other shrimp gobies if hiding places are in short supply. It may be bullied by larger, more aggressive species (especially those that hang out on or near the aquarium bottom). Keep only one in a smaller tank (unless you can acquire a pair) or if you have a tank of 55 gallons or larger. It will not bother invertebrate tankmates.
AQUARIUM BEHAVIOR: The Redbanded Shrimp Goby will live in a burrow with a snapping shrimp (try to obtain the Tiger Snapping Shrimp, *Alpheus bellulus*). It serves as a lookout and hunter for the shrimp, which provides them both with a protective burrow. It will jump out of an open aquarium when harassed or if it cannot find a suitable hiding place.

SPOTTAIL SHRIMP GOBY *Amblyeleotris latifasciata*
(Metallic Shrimp Goby)

MAXIMUM LENGTH: 6.3 in. (16 cm).

NATIVE RANGE: West Pacific.

MINIMUM AQUARIUM: Size: 30 gal. (114 L).

OVERVIEW: This is a beautifully marked member of the shrimp goby clan and one that is easy to keep. If possible, try to acquire it with an appropriate snapping shrimp so you can watch the pair in action.

FEEDING: Carnivore. Feed meaty fresh and frozen foods—which will be eaten by both fish and shrimp—at least once a day.

HABITAT: Reef-sand interface. Provide some burrows or holes near the aquarium bottom where this fish can hide if you do not keep it with its partner shrimp.

COMPATIBILITY: It is not typically hostile toward any tank residents, although it may challenge and duel with other shrimp gobies, especially if hiding places are limited in number. It is a larger species, so it is more likely to dominate smaller, related species (like the Redbanded Shrimp Goby, *A. fasciata*). Keep one per tank, unless you can acquire a known heterosexual pair (it is difficult to sex these fish with the naked eye). If your tank is large (100 gallons or more) it may be possible to keep two individuals of unknown sex together. It will not harm invertebrates.

AQUARIUM BEHAVIOR: Keeping this fish with its crustacean partner can provide many hours of viewing entertainment. The goby will stand guard at the burrow entrance as the shrimp pushes sand out of the burrow. It may jump out of an open tank when startled.

YELLOW CLOWN GOBY *Gobiodon okinawae*
(Yellow Coral Goby, Okinawa Goby)

MAXIMUM LENGTH: 1.4 in. (3.6 cm).

NATIVE RANGE: West Pacific.

MINIMUM AQUARIUM SIZE: 10 gal. (38 L).

OVERVIEW: This lemon-colored species is a member of a fascinating genus that always lives and breeds within branching stony coral colonies. The fish is thought to repay its coral host by providing water circulation and nutrients in the form of its wastes, which are taken up by the coral polyps.

FEEDING: Carnivore. Feed meaty foods at least once a day.

HABITAT: Reef, usually with *Acropora* coral colonies. Provide plenty of hiding places, which can be live or faux species of branching stony corals.

COMPATIBILITY: The Yellow Clown Goby is a mellow fish. It will ignore other species (with the exception of other small gobies that try to invade its coral home). Because of its small size, it may be picked on by dottybacks and aggressive damselfishes. However, it produces an unpalatable mucus that deters many predators. You can keep more than one in the same tank if there are enough suitable hiding places (e.g., live or faux branching coral colonies). They may clear some polyps from a stony coral branch to use as a site to lay their eggs.

AQUARIUM BEHAVIOR: This is a secretive little fish that will remain among the branches of a stony coral. It sometimes hovers above its home and will dash out to snatch passing food particles. It has been known to spawn in the home aquarium.

YELLOW SHRIMP GOBY *Cryptocentrus cinctus*
(Banded Shrimp Goby, Yellow Watchman Goby, Yellow Prawn Goby)

MAXIMUM LENGTH: 3.9 in. (10 cm).

NATIVE RANGE: Indo-West Pacific.

MINIMUM AQUARIUM SIZE: 10 gal. (38 L).

OVERVIEW: This is a wonderful shrimp goby that comes in a variety of different color morphs—yellow, gray or brown, with blue spots. Sometimes available as a mated pair with a commensal shrimp to share their den.

FEEDING: Carnivore. Feed meaty fresh and frozen foods—which will be eaten by both fish and shrimp—at least once a day.

HABITAT: Reef-sand interface. Provide some burrows or holes near the aquarium bottom where this fish can hide if you do not keep it with its partner shrimp.

COMPATIBILITY: This species will not bother unrelated fish species. However, it may fight with other gobies, especially if space is limited. If you keep it with other shrimp gobies, be sure that all tank residents have appropriate places to hide so there is no bickering over shelter sites. It will fight with members of its own kind, unless the fish are members of the opposite sex or your tank is large enough for individuals to put some distance between one another. It is not a threat to ornamental invertebrates.

AQUARIUM BEHAVIOR: This goby will spend much of its time at the entrance of a preferred hole or burrow, whether it is kept with a snapping shrimp or not. It will rise off the bottom to snatch passing food items. They have been known to jump from an open aquarium.

ROYAL GRAMMA *Gramma loreto*
(Fairy Basslet)

MAXIMUM LENGTH: 3.1 in. (7.9 cm).

NATIVE RANGE: Tropical West Atlantic, Caribbean.

MINIMUM AQUARIUM SIZE: 15 gal. (57 L).

OVERVIEW: Here is an easy-to-keep, fun-to-watch cave-dwelling species that is much-loved by marine aquarists for its brilliant colors and relatively passive disposition.

FEEDING: Carnivore. Feed meaty foods at least once a day. Supplementation with color-enhancing rations will help maintain its vivid pigmentation.

HABITAT: Reef. Provide plenty of hiding places. It usually hovers under overhangs and in caves, often in an upside-down position with its belly toward the ceiling. It will make good use of these types of realistic habitats in the aquarium.

COMPATIBILITY: Not usually aggressive toward other species, it may fight with its own kind or other *Gramma* species. Place one per tank, unless the aquarium is large or you acquire a pair (no obvious sexual differences except males tend to be larger than females). The Royal Gramma may chase small zooplankton feeders (e.g., *Chromis*, certain gobies), but this is not a problem unless the tank is small.

AQUARIUM BEHAVIOR: Once it knows the lay of the land and finds suitable hiding places, the Royal Gramma will hover in the water column and pick off passing food particles. It may occasionally jump out of an open aquarium. Males are nest builders and spawning activity may occur. Captive-bred specimens are occasionally available.

BLUE HAMLET *Hypoplectrus gemma*

MAXIMUM LENGTH: 5.1 in. (13 cm).

NATIVE RANGE: South Florida, Bahamas, Belize.

MINIMUM AQUARIUM SIZE: 55 gal. (209 L).

OVERVIEW: This is one of a handful of bright blue fishes available in the aquarium trade and one that mimics the Blue Chromis (*Chromis cyanea*) in order to sneak up on its prey.

FEEDING: Carnivore. Feed a varied diet, including chopped seafood, live ghost shrimp, frozen preparations for carnivores, and frozen mysid shrimp. Feed at least once a day. Regular meals of color-enhancing foods are advised to prevent loss of its beautiful pigmentation.

HABITAT: Reef. This fish will need lots of hiding places, such as rocky caves and crevices, to feel secure in a captive system.

COMPATIBILITY: Although these fishes are rarely aggressive toward unrelated species, they are occasionally attacked by more belligerent fishes like other groupers, larger dottybacks, larger hawkfishes, larger damselfishes and triggerfishes. They will consume shrimp, crabs and smaller fishes. They can be kept in reef aquariums, but only one Blue Hamlet should be kept per tank. If you have a large aquarium, it is possible to keep two species of *Hypoplectrus* together.

AQUARIUM BEHAVIOR: Every time an adult individual is moved, it will have a more difficult time adjusting to its new captive environment. Hamlets that don't acclimate will hide constantly and refuse to feed. Larger hamlets are more prone to acclimation difficulties when transferred from one tank to another. This species is a simultaneous hermaphrodite, with each fish having both male and female organs.

CHALK BASS *Serranus tortugarum*

MAXIMUM LENGTH: 3.1 in. (8 cm).

NATIVE RANGE: Florida and Caribbean.

MINIMUM AQUARIUM SIZE: 20 gal. (76 L).

OVERVIEW: This very pretty little bass with brilliant color highlights is a passive plankton feeder that fits well in a peaceful community setting, or a Caribbean or Florida Keys biotope tank.

FEEDING: Carnivore. Feed meaty foods such as enriched adult brine shrimp or mysid shrimp twice a day. Pigment-enhancing enriched foods, offered at least several times each week, are recommended to sustain its lustrous colors.

HABITAT: Reef-sand interface. Provide this fish with plenty of hiding places. In nature, it is sometimes found living in empty conch shells or among coral and shell rubble.

COMPATIBILITY: It is best kept in small groups in the aquarium. Individuals will form dominance hierarchies, their rank in the pecking order being determined by their size. If you are keeping more than one Chalk Bass per aquarium, all individuals should be introduced simultaneously. It is a zooplankton feeder and will not bother corals, clams, crabs or most shrimp, with the possible exception of the tiny, delicate *Periclimenes* spp.

AQUARIUM BEHAVIOR: This species will spend much time in the open, often swimming high in the water column. The Chalk Bass is known to be a simultaneous hermaphrodite; that is, each fish has functional testes and ovaries, and when spawning each fish takes turns acting as a female and male.

CORAL HIND *Cephalopholis miniata*
(Miniata Grouper, Coral Grouper)

MAXIMUM LENGTH: 17.7 in. (45 cm).

NATIVE RANGE: Indo-Pacific.

MINIMUM AQUARIUM SIZE: 100 gal. (380 L).

OVERVIEW: This dazzling grouper has starred in countless reef calendars and is a commendable aquarium fish, virtually "bulletproof" and staying relatively small (for a grouper)—but still requiring a good-size home.

FEEDING: Carnivore. Feed chopped seafood and meaty dry and frozen preparations. Feed to satiation several times a week. Color-enhancing foods should be offered frequently. An occasional specimen may require live feeder ghost shrimp to initiate feeding.

HABITAT: Reef. Provide it with one (or more) good, sturdy cave or hiding place. Like all large carnivores, it produces lots of waste, and the tank will need an efficient protein skimmer and carbon filtration.

COMPATIBILITY: The Coral Hind is a voracious predator that will eat any fish or crustacean it can swallow (do not underestimate the size of its mouth or the speed with which it can attack). It is especially adept at ingesting long, skinny fish. (Lyretail Anthias are this species' favorite prey in the wild.) Keep one per tank, as conspecifics are likely to quarrel. It can be housed with other smaller groupers if the tank is extra large.

AQUARIUM BEHAVIOR: It can be rather reclusive when first added to the tank, but as time passes, it will become bolder (especially as it begins to recognize its keeper as a source of food).

SWISSGUARD BASSLET *Liopropoma rubre*
(Peppermint Bass)

MAXIMUM LENGTH: 3.1 in. (7.9 cm).
NATIVE RANGE: Tropical Western Atlantic, Florida and Caribbean.
MINIMUM AQUARIUM SIZE: 20 gal. (76 L).
OVERVIEW: The spectacular color pattern of this crevice-dweller makes it a welcome addition to the less-aggressive fish community. It's cryptic nature makes it difficult to spot (and catch) in the wild, making it a prized species among reef aquarists.
FEEDING: Carnivore. Feed meaty foods daily.
HABITAT: Reef. Provide an aquascape with rocky overhangs, crevices and caves to approximate its wild habitat.
COMPATIBILITY: A proficient predator, it will eat crustaceans and tiny fish tankmates (e.g., small gobies). It is not aggressive toward non-relatives (it may squabble over a favorite hiding place). It may be picked on by more aggressive substrate-bound fishes (dottybacks, hawkfishes, large damselfishes) causing the fish to hide most of the time. A pair can be kept in a small tank. Although difficult to sex, try getting a small and larger individual and add them simultaneously.
AQUARIUM BEHAVIOR: Extremely adept at hiding to avoid fish-eating predators, the Swissguard Basslet will spend more time in the open if the tank is kept in a quiet location of the home. Do not be surprised if you do not see it for a week or so (leave it alone and allow it to properly acclimate). It will spend much of its time hovering at the entrance to its den, ready to dart out and snap up passing food. It may leap from an open aquarium if startled.

ARC-EYE HAWKFISH *Paracirrhites arcatus*

MAXIMUM LENGTH: 5.5 in. (14 cm).

NATIVE RANGE: Indo-West Pacific.

MINIMUM AQUARIUM SIZE: 30 gal. (114 L).

OVERVIEW: Appearing in different color schemes and bedecked with distinctive orange eyeliner markings, this is a very handsome, durable member of the hawkfish clan. Like most other hawkfishes, it is an ambush predator, perching patiently on rocks or corals until an appropriate prey item comes within striking range. This species has a large mouth and is a potential threat to a variety of smaller tankmates. House it only with tankmates that can fend for themselves.

FEEDING: Carnivore. Feed meaty foods at least once a day.

HABITAT: Reef. It will rest on stony corals or live rock and duck into interstices when threatened.

COMPATIBILITY: The Arc-eye Hawkfish is a stocky, more aggressive hawkfish that will pick on smaller, benthic fishes. It may even harass more passive fishes of equal or slightly greater size added to the tank after it has become acclimated. This species can be kept in pairs, although sexing individuals can be difficult (attempt to keep two fish that are different in size in a larger tank). It will eat any fish or crustacean that it can swallow whole.

AQUARIUM BEHAVIOR: Spending most of its time in repose on the substrate, it will dash into the water column to snatch passing food items. It may jump from an open aquarium. It offers a fascinating glimpse into the life of a classic reef predator, with ever-alert eyes and fast hunting reflexes.

FALCO'S HAWKFISH *Cirrhitichthys falco*
(Pygmy, Pixie or Dwarf Hawkfish, Redspotted Hawkfish)

MAXIMUM LENGTH: 3.1 in. (7.9 cm).

NATIVE RANGE: Indo-Pacific.

MINIMUM AQUARIUM SIZE: 10 gal. (38 L).

OVERVIEW: This is a comical, personable little fish that spends much of its time perching in the open, alertly watching for danger or feeding opportunities. Its dorsal spines present a dressy image, with tuft-like filaments projecting from each tip.

FEEDING: Carnivore. Feed meaty foods at least once a day. Color-enhancing rations will help prevent color loss.

HABITAT: Reef, usually in association with stony coral colonies.

COMPATIBILITY: It may pester some small, nonaggressive fishes (dartfishes, small gobies, some anthias, flasher wrasses and other small, inoffensive wrasses), especially in smaller quarters. In an aquarium with less aggressive species, it should be the last fish introduced. In contrast, this hawkfish is often bullied by other hawkfishes and more aggressive fish tankmates. It should be the first fish added to a tank that is going to contain more pugnacious species. Falco's Hawkfish is one of the better species for the reef aquarium, as its smaller size makes it less of a threat to ornamental crustaceans. Males tend to be larger than females.

AQUARIUM BEHAVIOR: Its swimming is largely restricted to bursts of movement, and it presents a droll image, with its prominent eyes brightly scanning the surrounding environs for food or rivals. It may jump from an open tank if harassed or startled.

LONGNOSE HAWKFISH *Oxycirrhites typus*

MAXIMUM LENGTH: 5.1 (13 cm).

NATIVE RANGE: Indo-Pacific, Red Sea to West Coast of Colombia.

MINIMUM AQUARIUM SIZE: 20 gal. (76 L).

OVERVIEW: This checkerboard-patterned hawkfish is a durable and captivating aquarium resident. It has an elongate snout that is used to extract shrimp from reef crevices, but it also feeds on planktonic crustaceans and even small fishes.

FEEDING: Carnivore. Feed meaty foods, including mysid shrimp and enriched brine shrimp, at least once a day.

HABITAT: Reef. The Longnose Hawkfish often perches among gorgonian branches or on live rock. It should be provided with a number of suitable hiding places.

COMPATIBILITY: Longnose Hawkfish of the same sex will often fight if placed together. Fighting often consists of jaw-locking and can result in injury (combatants should be separated). They can be kept in male-female pairs. It will eat ornamental shrimps and small fishes. It grasps prey that are too large in its jaws and busts them to pieces by bashing them against hard structure. It has a propensity to pester more elongate fishes (dartfish, worm gobies).

AQUARIUM BEHAVIOR: In typical hawkfish hunting mode, this fish perches on rocks or corals (often on sea fans in the wild) and swiftly ambushes prey that comes into its striking range. This species most often perishes as a result of leaping from open tanks or from small holes in the aquarium top. Be sure the tank is well-covered.

LYRETAIL HAWKFISH *Cyprinocirrhites polyactis*
(Pink Hawkfish, Swallowtail Hawkfish)

MAXIMUM LENGTH: 5.5 in. (14 cm).

NATIVE RANGE: Indo-West Pacific.

MINIMUM AQUARIUM SIZE: 20 gal. (76 L).

OVERVIEW: This oddball of the hawkfish family spends much of its time in the wild feeding on plankton in the water column, acting more like an anthias than a member of a family known for perching rather than swimming. Its prominent eyes are a deep blue or green, depending on your angle of view.

FEEDING: Carnivore. Feed meaty foods, such as mysid shrimp and enriched adult brine shrimp, at least twice a day.

HABITAT: Reef. Provide suitable hiding places. May also live among the tentacles or at the base of some larger sea anemones. Responds well to the presence of strong currents in the aquarium.

COMPATIBILITY: Although not as aggressive as most other hawkfishes, it will often chastise smaller tankmates. It might also behave aggressively toward more passive fishes that are introduced after it is an established resident with its territory staked out. Keeping more than one *C. polyactis* in anything smaller than a large aquarium is risky. Males will fight, although a single male will tolerate female conspecifics.

AQUARIUM BEHAVIOR: This species will spend most of its time in repose, unless the system pump provides a considerable amount of water movement, in which case it will often swim against the current up in the water column.

YELLOWHEAD JAWFISH *Opistognathus aurifrons*
(Pearly Jawfish)

MAXIMUM LENGTH: 3.9 in. (10 cm).

NATIVE RANGE: Tropical West-Atlantic, Caribbean.

MINIMUM AQUARIUM SIZE: 20 gal. (76 L).

OVERVIEW: These comical fish are luminously beautiful and put on a constant show of interesting behaviors, especially if kept in colonies.

FEEDING: Carnivore. Feed meaty foods at least twice daily.

HABITAT: Sand and rubble. Provide a 4-inch (10 cm) deep bed of mixed substrate consisting of sand, coral or rocky rubble, and bits of shell to facilitate burrow construction. Jawfishes will often dig under a flat rock placed on the sand, using it as a roof for their burrow chamber. Provide plenty of open sand bottom.

COMPATIBILITY: Jawfishes are best housed with more passive fish species, especially in a smaller tank. They perform best in groups, and it is advisable to add all the individuals at once. A good rule of thumb is approximately 2 to 2.5 square feet per individual. This species will chase smaller fishes away from its burrow, but rarely harms tank-mates. Aggressive fishes (dottybacks, some of the pygmy angelfishes, triggerfishes) may pester jawfishes. Many predatory fishes (eels, frog-fishes, groupers) will eat these fish.

AQUARIUM BEHAVIOR: This species is a burrow builder, digging by taking mouthfuls of substrate and spitting the debris at the burrow entrance. The jawfish will hover near its lair or rest in its entrance waiting for food items to pass. It is also a jumper and an expert at finding small holes in the aquarium cover from which to leap.

COMMON LIONFISH *Pterois volitans*
(Volitans Lionfish, Black Volitans Lionfish, Red Lionfish)

MAXIMUM LENGTH: 15 in. (38 cm).

NATIVE RANGE: Indo-West Pacific.

MINIMUM AQUARIUM SIZE: 75 gal. (285 L).

OVERVIEW: This is a great aquarium species, exceptionally hardy and providing a constant display as it parades about the tank. Beware, as its fin spines are loaded with a potent venom.

FEEDING: Carnivore. Feed meaty seafoods, such as shrimp and squid, to satiation several times a week. To start a new fish feeding, offer fresh seafood from the end of a feeding stick. If the lionfish shows no interest, live ghost shrimp or feeder fish are rarely rejected.

HABITAT: Reef or reef-sand interface, lagoons. It tends to stay in the open and needs ample room to swim in and rest.

COMPATIBILITY: This ornate creature is not usually a threat to any tankmate, except for those that will fit into its extended jaws. On rare occasions, it may behave aggressively toward another lionfish— during such battles it may joust at its opponent with its venomous dorsal spines. It will eat smaller fishes and ornamental shrimps.

AQUARIUM BEHAVIOR: Because of its boldness, it is one of the best of the lionfishes for life in the aquarium. It will learn to recognize its keeper as a source of food, and will beg at the water's surface when it sees him or her in the room. Give its venomous spines plenty of space when cleaning the aquarium, and be sure children cannot reach into the tank. Stings are painful, but not lethal, although allergic reactions are potentially severe.

ZEBRA LIONFISH *Dendrochirus zebra*
(Dwarf Lionfish, Zebra Turkeyfish)

MAXIMUM LENGTH: 7 in. (18 cm).
NATIVE RANGE: Indo-West Pacific, Red Sea.
MINIMUM AQUARIUM SIZE: 30 gal. (114 L).
OVERVIEW: A showy member of the scorpionfish family, this species remains relatively small and is easier to house than its relatives. Note that its spines can deliver a dose of venom, so it must be treated with caution and respect. Wounds are painful, sometimes excruciating, to humans, but no fatalities have been reported.
FEEDING: Carnivore. Feed with meaty seafoods, such as shrimp or squid. Attempt to feed fresh seafood from the end of a feeding stick. To get a new specimen eating, live gut-packed ghost shrimp or feeder fish may be needed. Feed to satiation several times a week.
HABITAT: Reef, with stony corals or among coral rubble. Provide a sheltering cave or crevice in the aquarium.
COMPATIBILITY: Larger individuals may fight with their own kind and related lionfish. Combat often includes jabbing its opponent with its dorsal spines (this is not typically lethal to the recipient of the sting). It will eat smaller fishes and crustaceans. Aquarists must handle this species with great care and block children's access to the tank.
AQUARIUM BEHAVIOR: During the day, this lionfish is fairly inactive, usually tucking into coral crevices. It may hide until light levels are lowered or when live food is added to the tank. When it stalks a ghost shrimp or feeder fish, it will use its large pectoral fins to block the escape route of its quarry.

SNOWFLAKE MORAY *Echidna nebulosa*

MAXIMUM LENGTH: 39.3 in. (100 cm).

NATIVE RANGE: Indo-Pacific, Eastern Pacific (Baja to Colombia).

MINIMUM AQUARIUM SIZE: 30 gal. (114 L).

OVERVIEW: This is a pleasingly marked, extremely hardy and long-lived fish that readily acclimates to aquarium life and is the ideal choice for a first marine eel. It does not share the large size or aggressive fish-eating traits of the more notorious members of its family.

FEEDING: Carnivore. Feed fresh or frozen seafood, such as shrimp or pieces of non-oily fish (live food may be required for some individuals). Feed to satiation several times a week.

HABITAT: Reef. Provide lots of caves and crevices. Without such structures, it is likely to swim about the tank continually and stop feeding, and may leap from the tank if it can find an exit.

COMPATIBILITY: This moray feeds primarily on crabs and shrimp in the wild, and is not as big a threat to fish tankmates as some of its relatives. However, it may consume smaller fishes and is especially prone to feeding on crustaceans. Larger morays have been known to eat this eel.

AQUARIUM BEHAVIOR: The Snowflake Moray will spend much of its time with its head protruding from a crevice. When food enters the water, it leaves its refuge and swims about searching for the source of the attractive odors. In this excited state, it may occasionally nip at fish tankmates. The aquarist can curtail this behavior, to some degree, by delivering its meal on a feeding stick. The aquarium must be carefully covered, as all eels are prone to slithering up and out of their tanks.

SPINY PUFFER *Diodon holocanthus*
(Porcupinefish, Balloon Porcupinefish, Longspine Porcupinefish)

MAXIMUM LENGTH: 11.8 in. (30 cm).

NATIVE RANGE: Circumtropical.

MINIMUM AQUARIUM SIZE: 75 gal. (285 L).

OVERVIEW: A comical-looking species with a wonderful personality, these inflatable fish make fascinating pets. They are greedy eaters, rising up to take food from their keepers' fingers.

FEEDING: Omnivore, but primarily a carnivore in the wild. Feed meaty and herbivore foods twice a day.

HABITAT: Reef or reef-sand interface, lagoons and seagrass beds. Provide ample swimming space as well a rocky hiding places.

COMPATIBILITY: These puffers are not typically a threat to other fishes. However, they may nip at those species with elaborate finnage, fishes that resemble the substrate or species that cannot move very fast. They do not usually bother one another, although it is best to add them to the tank all at once. This fish is a potential threat to a number of different invertebrates, including worms, snails, clams, sea stars and sea urchins. It can be kept with unpalatable soft corals.

AQUARIUM BEHAVIOR: The Spiny Puffer spends much of its time resting on the substrate or begging for food. Once it learns to associate its keeper with food, it will swim along the front glass and eye the aquarist as he or she approaches the aquarium. When threatened or sometimes for no apparent reason, these fish will inflate with water. If they are out of the water, they may inflate with air, which can be lethal, as the fish may have difficulty expelling the ingested air. Never remove a puffer from the water to see it inflate.

FOXFACE RABBITFISH *Siganus vulpinus*
(Foxface)

MAXIMUM LENGTH: 9.4 in. (24 cm).

NATIVE RANGE: West Pacific.

MINIMUM AQUARIUM SIZE: 100 gal. (380 L).

OVERVIEW: Rabbitfishes are terrific marine aquarium community members, and this species is a strikingly colored algae-eating machine that is hardy and a valuable aquarium resident. Beware of its venomous fin spines that can cause painful stings.

FEEDING: Herbivore. Offer fresh, dried or frozen algae-based foods at least three times a day. You may be able to feed it less if there is a good algal crop in the aquarium.

HABITAT: Reef and lagoons with sheltering coral growth. Provide suitable hiding places, as well as swimming room.

COMPATIBILITY: This rabbitfish will not behave aggressively toward other fishes, but may occasionally chase other herbivores (especially tangs) and it may quarrel with other rabbitfishes. It is best to keep one per tank, unless you can acquire a pair or have a very large tank (180 gallons [684 L] or more). They are often used in reef tanks to control algae and are typically well-behaved—however, the occasional individual may nip at and even eat large-polyped stony corals or mushroom anemones.

AQUARIUM BEHAVIOR: This is an active fish that roams about the aquarium looking for grazing opportunities. When stressed or at night it will adopt a dark mottling coloration over its body. Initially, it will be nervous in its new home, but will mellow and show its true, beautiful colors as time goes on. Always handle with caution.

REDSPOTTED SANDPERCH *Parapercis schauinslandii*
(Schauinsland's Sandperch)

MAXIMUM LENGTH: 5.1 in. (13 cm).

NATIVE RANGE: Indo-Pacific.

MINIMUM AQUARIUM SIZE: 55 gal. (209 L).

OVERVIEW: This is a droll-looking, attractively marked fish that spends its time hopping about on the aquarium substrate.

FEEDING: Carnivore. Feed meaty seafoods at least twice a day.

HABITAT: Reef-sand interface. Provide hiding places on the aquarium bottom. (Ideally, make a depression in the sand and place a flat rock over it, leaving an entrance hole for the sandperch.)

COMPATIBILITY: This species will quarrel with species that live on the aquarium bottom and that have a similar body plan (more elongate). Gobies, for example, are a frequent target. In many cases, however, the sandperch itself is the target of more aggressive species like larger damselfishes, larger dottybacks and hawkfishes. Keep only one per small to moderate-size tank—if the tank is large enough (e.g., 135 gallons [513 L] or more) it is possible to keep two individuals in the same tank. Select juveniles or two individuals that differ in size so it is more likely that you will acquire a heterosexual pair. It is not a threat to corals, but will eat worms, shrimps and crabs.

AQUARIUM BEHAVIOR: This fish will spend its time resting on the bottom, hopping from one place to another, sometimes shooting up into the water column to grab a piece of food. It will jump out of an open tank if startled. Be sure the aquarium is always covered.

SIX-STRIPED SOAPFISH *Grammistes sexlineatus*
(Six-line Soapfish, Goldlined Soapfish)

MAXIMUM LENGTH: 11.8 in. (30 cm).

NATIVE RANGE: Indo-Pacific, Red Sea.

MINIMUM AQUARIUM SIZE: 55 gal. (209 L).

OVERVIEW: Not for everyone, this is a handsome fish and an interesting choice for the aquarist looking for an unusual, highly predatory aquarium inhabitant. It produces a toxic slime (it will actually lather in a bucket), but this is rarely a problem. Color patterns change considerably as the fish grows, from two stripes on young juveniles to six as a subadult and a series of broken lines on adults.

FEEDING: Carnivore. Satiate with meaty foods, such as shrimp, squid or non-oily marine fish flesh twice a week.

HABITAT: Reef and rocky coastal waters. Suitable caves and overhangs are required to make this fish feel at home.

COMPATIBILITY: Two words: eating machine. It is the "über-predator," consuming any fish or crustacean that fits in its mouth and even tankmates that are too large to swallow. (They are known to swim around with part of a damsel or shrimp protruding from their mouths for hours, waiting to swallow.) Keep one per tank. Large individuals will not hesitate to eat smaller Six-striped Soapfish.

AQUARIUM BEHAVIOR: At first, this soapfish will hide most of the time, sneaking about the tank and peeking out from hiding places. But once it begins to see its keeper as a food source, it will become a true pet, begging for handouts and swimming back and forth at the front of the tank when the aquarist enters the room.

PURPLE TANG *Zebrasoma xanthurum*
(Yellowtail Tang)

MAXIMUM LENGTH: 9.8 in. (25 cm).

NATIVE RANGE: Red Sea, Western Indian Ocean.

MINIMUM AQUARIUM SIZE: 100 gal. (380 L).

OVERVIEW: Here is a magnificent Red Sea beauty that was once rare and breathtakingly expensive, but is now readily available in the aquarium trade and is often used to help control algae growth.

FEEDING: Herbivore. Offer algae-based foods at least three times a day, as well as freeze-dried algae flakes or sheets of seaweed (nori). If it has lush live algae in the tank, it may require less feeding.

HABITAT: Reef. Provide several larger caves or crevices in which it can shelter when threatened. It also needs plenty of swimming room.

COMPATIBILITY: This is a rather aggressive tang that is particularly intolerant of members of its own genus or other algae-eating species. While it usually ignores bottom-dwelling species, it is likely to attack fishes with similar shape or behaviors. It will use the sharp spine at the front of the tail to slash at fishes or aquarists it perceives as a threat. It is prudent to keep one per tank unless the system is extra large. Although it often causes no problems in the reef aquarium, it has been known to nip clam mantles and large-polyped stony corals—especially if food is in short supply.

AQUARIUM BEHAVIOR: This vividly colored fish usually acclimates readily to aquarium life, spending more time in the open as it gradually becomes accustomed to its new home. If startled, it will dash into a bolt hole, but will soon reappear.

SAILFIN TANG *Zebrasoma veliferum*

MAXIMUM LENGTH: 15.7 in. (40 cm).

NATIVE RANGE: Pacific Ocean.

MINIMUM AQUARIUM SIZE: 135 gal. (513 L).

OVERVIEW: A showy species with large, sail-like dorsal and anal fins and a pleasing banded color pattern, this fish will help control algae growth in the aquarium. (The very similar Red Sea Sailfin Tang is known as *Zebrasoma desjardani*.)

FEEDING: Herbivore. Feed algae-based rations at least three times a day, as well as freeze-dried algae and/or dried seaweed (nori). You may be able to feed it less if there is a good algal crop in the aquarium. Regular offerings of color-enhancing foods will help prevent fading of its pigmentation.

HABITAT: Reef or reef-sand interface. Provide it with plenty of bolt holes and lots of open swimming space.

COMPATIBILITY: This tends to be one of the most amicable members of the tang (surgeonfish) clan. Although an adult that is established in a tank may let newly added fish know where they fit into the pecking order (especially other tang), it rarely causes problems. It is best to keep one per tank, unless you have a larger aquarium. It rarely bothers invertebrates, although the occasional specimen may develop the bad habit of nipping at clam mantles or the polyps of fleshy large-polyped stony corals.

AQUARIUM BEHAVIOR: This is a very active fish that will spend most of its time in the open grazing on algae. It will become rather tame, accepting food from its keeper's fingers.

YELLOW TANG *Zebrasoma flavescens*

MAXIMUM LENGTH: 7.9 in. (20 cm).

NATIVE RANGE: Central and South Pacific.

MINIMUM AQUARIUM SIZE: 75 gal. (285 L).

OVERVIEW: A marine aquarium classic, this is a brilliant yellow, stunning fish—collected mostly from Hawaiian waters—that can help keep certain types of troublesome algae in check.

FEEDING: Herbivore. Feed algae-based foods at least three times a day, as well as freeze-dried algae flakes or seaweed sheets (nori). You may be able to feed it less if there is a good algal crop in the aquarium.

HABITAT: Reef and lagoons with protective coral growth. Provide several larger caves or crevices in which it can shelter when threatened. It also needs plenty of swimming room.

COMPATIBILITY: This fish can be cranky toward other herbivores, especially in crowded confines. Once placed in a tank, it usually does not take a Yellow Tang long to establish the whole aquarium as its territory. Keep just one per tank, unless the aquarium is large (180 gallons [684 L] or more), in which case you should add three or more individuals simultaneously. It is rarely a threat to clams and corals.

AQUARIUM BEHAVIOR: The Yellow Tang will swim about the tank inspecting all surfaces for algae on which to browse. If it is not getting proper nutrition, the stomach will look pinched, and it may suffer from erosion of the skin around the head and the fins. It can use is scalpel-sharp tangs (seen as white spines at the base of the tail) to inflict wounds on other fishes (or careless fishkeepers). The downside—it is particularly susceptible to parasites.

BLUECHIN TRIGGERFISH *Xanthichthys auromarginatus*
(Gilded Triggerfish)

MAXIMUM LENGTH: 8.7 in. (22 cm).

NATIVE RANGE: Indo-Pacific.

MINIMUM AQUARIUM SIZE: 75 gal. (285 L).

OVERVIEW: This personable triggerfish is bold and beautiful and can even be kept in a reef tank. It often becomes a favorite pet.

FEEDING: Omnivore. Feed meaty and algae-based foods several times a day.

HABITAT: Reef or reef-sand interface. Provide several suitable hiding places, as well as plenty of swimming room.

COMPATIBILITY: This is one of the better-behaved triggerfishes. It can be kept with fish tankmates of similar size and can even be housed with smaller fishes (the latter should be added to the tank first). If it gets too hungry, however, it may attempt to intercept and eat more diminutive fish tankmates. It is likely to be bullied by more aggressive triggerfishes, but can usually hold its own with most other tankmates. A male and female can be kept in the same tank (females lack the blue patch on the chin). It is not a threat to corals, but may eat ornamental shrimps.

AQUARIUM BEHAVIOR: While it tends to be reclusive when first added to the tank, this triggerfish soon learns to associate the aquarist with food. Many individuals will beg for food at the front of the tank and may even spit water at the aquarium top or out of the tank (be sure these jets of water cannot reach electrical outlets). On rare occasions, it may jump from an open tank.

NIGER TRIGGERFISH *Odonus niger*
(Redtooth Triggerfish)

MAXIMUM LENGTH: 19.7 in. (50 cm), including long tail filaments.

NATIVE RANGE: Indo-Pacific.

MINIMUM AQUARIUM SIZE: 100 gal. (380 L).

OVERVIEW: An active, showy member of the triggerfish clan that sports red-pigmented teeth that protrude from the jaws as an adult.

FEEDING: Omnivore. Feed meaty and herbivore foods several times a day. Meals of color-enhancing foods several times each week will be beneficial.

HABITAT: Reef. Provide several good crevices for this species to slide into, as well as plenty of swimming room.

COMPATIBILITY: The Niger Triggerfish is not a particularly combative fish and does not usually bother other fishes in an aquarium setting. It may occasionally pester small fishes that are added to a tank where it already resides. You can keep more than one in the same large tank—add all individuals simultaneously. This is one triggerfish that causes few problems in the reef aquarium. Some individuals may attack and eat ornamental shrimps, and they may turn on some sessile invertebrates if they are not fed often enough.

AQUARIUM BEHAVIOR: The Niger Triggerfish is an active species that will scull about the tank looking for tasty morsels. It will rapidly retreat into a crevice, headfirst, when threatened, and only back out when it feels the danger has passed. It has been known to rearrange aquarium decor by lifting pieces of the reef in its jaws or blowing jets of water at the soft substrate.

PICASSO TRIGGERFISH *Rhinecanthus aculeatus*
(Humu Humu Triggerfish, Blackbar Triggerfish)

MAXIMUM LENGTH: 9.8 in. (25 cm).

NATIVE RANGE: Indo-West Pacific.

MINIMUM AQUARIUM SIZE: 75 gal. (285 L).

OVERVIEW: The legendary Hawaiian Humu-humu-nuku-nuku-apua'a makes a fascinating pet. It readily adapts to aquarium living and will delight its owner with its interesting behaviors, even making a soft grunting noise when threatened.

FEEDING: Omnivore. Feed meaty seafoods, as well as herbivore rations several times a day.

HABITAT: Reef-sand interface with lots of rubble. Provide several good hiding crevices and adequate swimming room.

COMPATIBILITY: The Picasso Trigger can be a bit of an underwater enigma. Some individuals behave perfectly with tankmates, while others change personalities and attempt to destroy smaller or more passive species. Some more peace-loving individuals may also snap and start harassing their subordinates. That said, it can be kept with other large, potentially aggressive, species. Juveniles are more passive than adults. and it is less of a threat to its neighbors in a larger tank. It will eat a wide range of ornamental invertebrates—thus, the reef aquarium is not a good home for this fish.

AQUARIUM BEHAVIOR: This is an active fish that always seems to be trying to figure out how to find another meal. It will lift coral rubble and shells as it searches for hidden prey, and may even rest on its side and use its pectoral fin to dig in the sand.

PINKTAIL TRIGGERFISH *Melichthys vidua*

MAXIMUM LENGTH: 13.8 in. (35 cm).

NATIVE RANGE: Indo-Pacific.

MINIMUM AQUARIUM SIZE: 100 gal. (380 L).

OVERVIEW: Here is one of the more peace-loving triggerfishes and one that can be housed with other large fishes. It may even be safely added to a reef aquarium.

FEEDING: Omnivore. Feed meaty seafoods and rations containing algae several times a day. Enriched, pigment-enhancing foods will help bring out its attractive coloration.

HABITAT: Reef. Provide ample swimming room with a couple of good hiding places that it can slide into.

COMPATIBILITY: This trigger is usually very tolerant of its piscine neighbors, but it may chase smaller, newly added fishes. Do not keep more than one Pinktail Triggerfish in the same tank, unless the aquarium is sizeable (180 gallons [684 L] or larger) or you can acquire a known male-female pair. It will usually ignore sessile invertebrates, but may occasionally succumb to the temptation of a shrimp snack.

AQUARIUM BEHAVIOR: This fish will become a bold aquarium resident with time. When threatened, it will duck quickly into a crevice and erect its dorsal spine (the "trigger" in a triggerfish), making it almost impossible to extract. It can be a spitter, blowing jets of water at the water's surface when begging for food. Most aquarists find this behavior amusing, but you may need to keep lights covered to avoid short-circuiting electrical outlets.

SCIMITAR TRIGGERFISH *Sufflamen bursa*
(Bursa Triggerfish, Scythe Triggerfish)

MAXIMUM LENGTH: 9.4 in. (24 cm).

NATIVE RANGE: Indo-Pacific.

MINIMUM AQUARIUM SIZE: 75 gal. (285 L).

OVERVIEW: Although the colors are more muted than those of some others in the family, this is a hardy, handsome fish that is loaded with personality.

FEEDING: Omnivore. Feed meaty and herbivore foods several times a day.

HABITAT: Reef-sand interface with lots of rubble. Provide several good hiding crevices and adequate swimming room.

COMPATIBILITY: Although this is a relatively peaceful member of the clan, it may throw its weight around and bully smaller fishes or more passive species introduced after it is well established in the tank. Young fish are more mild-mannered than their adult kin. Only one should be housed per tank, although it can be kept with other triggerfishes in a large aquarium. Reef aquarists should avoid this beast—it has a catholic diet that includes a diversity of ornamental invertebrate species.

AQUARIUM BEHAVIOR: While shy initially, the Scimitar Triggerfish will gradually adjust to its new environment, becoming bolder as it begins to recognize the aquarist as a source of sustenance. It will slide into crevices and cracks in or behind the reef when threatened. Although not common, this fish can jump from an open tank if startled or harassed.

BIRD WRASSE *Gomphosus varius*
(Green Bird Wrasse, Brown Bird Wrasse)

MAXIMUM LENGTH: 11 in. (28 cm).

NATIVE RANGE: Indo-Pacific.

MINIMUM AQUARIUM SIZE: 100 gal. (380 L).

OVERVIEW: A true oddity, this long-nosed wrasse is almost "bullet-proof" and able to survive less-than-ideal water conditions. Males are a glorious blue-green and females have brownish scales. It swoops through its environment like a bird in flight.

FEEDING: Carnivore. Feed meaty foods at least several times a day. Because it is so active, it is prone to losing weight if not fed enough.

HABITAT: Reef or reef-sand interface. This athletic creature needs lots of open, swimming space.

COMPATIBILITY: Do not let the long snout fool you—its mouth is relatively large and it will eat any fish that it can catch and swallow. Keep one male per tank, but a male and female can be kept together. Its catholic diet makes it a threat to a wide range of ornamental invertebrates (including feather dusters, snails, small clams, shrimps, crabs, brittlestars, sea stars, and small urchins).

AQUARIUM BEHAVIOR: This is a very active species that will pace from one end of the aquarium to the other. It will occasionally stop to probe a reef crevice with its snout or examine the bottom as it searches for food. As it grows, it is not uncommon for male Bird Wrasses to develop large bumps on the snout. These protuberances, which may be fatty tumors, do not tend to interfere with the feeding and general health of the Bird Wrasse.

BLUEHEAD FAIRY WRASSE *Cirrhilabrus cyanopleura*
(Yellowflanked Fairy Wrasse, Bluescaled Fairy Wrasse)

MAXIMUM LENGTH: 5.1 in. (13 cm).

NATIVE RANGE: Indo-West Pacific.

MINIMUM AQUARIUM SIZE: 55 gal. (209 L).

OVERVIEW: This is one of a number of amazing smaller, shoaling wrasses that exhibit striking colors and that readily adapt to certain aquarium venues.

FEEDING: Carnivore. Feed meaty foods such as mysid shrimp and enriched brine shrimp several times per day.

HABITAT: Reef. Good shelter sites are a must to ensure acclimation of the fairy wrasses. They may occasionally live among the tentacles of large-polyped stony corals. They need plenty of swimming room.

COMPATIBILITY: This species is rarely aggressive toward fish tankmates with the possible exception of its cousins. Once a male has fully acclimated to aquarium living, it may chase and nip at other fairy wrasses or the closely related flasher wrasses. You can keep more than one Bluehead Fairy Wrasse in the same tank, but add only one male per aquarium and one or more females. It is safe with most reef aquarium invertebrates.

AQUARIUM BEHAVIOR: This interesting fish often pops up and down as it moves through the water, in part because of its using its pectoral fins to scull through the water. It is a very accomplished escape artist that will leap from an open aquarium when startled or involved in courtship. It usually feeds from the water column, hunting zooplankton, although it will also pick some food off the substrate.

BLUEHEAD WRASSE *Thalassoma bifasciatum*

MAXIMUM LENGTH: 7.1 in. (18 cm).

NATIVE RANGE: Tropical Western Atlantic, Caribbean.

MINIMUM AQUARIUM SIZE: 75 gal. (285 L).

OVERVIEW: This active, eyecatching fish will add swooping flights of swimming action as well as color to the aquarium.

FEEDING: Carnivore. Feed meaty foods, several times a day.

HABITAT: Reef. Swimming space is very important as is the availablity of rocky nooks where it can dive into shelter. Juveniles will live among the tentacles of the Pink-tipped Sea Anemone *(Condylactis gigantea)*.

COMPATIBILITY: Initial phase individuals (which are yellow and can be juveniles, females or males) are usually amicable, but terminal phase males (green with a blue head) may chase smaller zooplankton feeders (small anthias, flasher wrasses, firefishes, dart gobies). Keep only one terminal male per tank, but you can house the initial phase fish together and/or with a single male. In some cases, yellow-phased individuals may change into terminal males. While young fish are not a threat to most ornamental invertebrates, adults may eat shrimps, small crabs, a variety of worms, and serpent stars.

AQUARIUM BEHAVIOR: The Bluehead Wrasse is a very active species that will dash about the aquarium. In a small tank, it will swim incessantly from one end of the tank to the other. It will feed out of the water column and off the substrate. Rather than bury under the sand, it hides in reef crevices during the night. This species is a real jumper —an aquarium top is a must.

EIGHTLINE WRASSE *Pseudocheilinus octotaenia*

MAXIMUM LENGTH: 5.3 in. (13 cm).

NATIVE RANGE: Indo-West Pacific.

MINIMUM AQUARIUM SIZE: 30 gal. (114 L).

OVERVIEW: This is a modest-size wrasse that is relatively durable and attractively marked, yet capable of combative behavior, especially in smaller aquariums.

FEEDING: Carnivore. Feed meaty foods, twice a day. Will require less frequent feeding in a reef tank with a healthy micro-invertebrate population.

HABITAT: Reef. Numerous hiding places are a must to keep this species happy and healthy.

COMPATIBILITY: Larger than its close cousin the Sixline Wrasse, this species is also a greater threat to its piscine neighbors. Do not keep it with more docile, smaller species in anything but a larger aquarium (135 gallons [513 L] or more). Larger adults will eat smaller, more elongated fishes. Younger Eightline Wrasse are less of a problem than their larger brethren. Do not keep more than one of these beasts in the same tank. In a very large tank (180 gallons [684 L] or more) you might add two juveniles or individuals that are disparate in size. This fish will eat ornamental crustaceans, but is not a threat to corals.

AQUARIUM BEHAVIOR: This is a rather cryptic species that likes to hang out at the entrance of crevices and caves. It will move into the open to snap up morsels of food. This species will spend more time hiding until it gets used to its new home.

EXQUISITE FAIRY WRASSE *Cirrhilabrus exquisitus*

MAXIMUM LENGTH: 4.7 in. (12 cm).

NATIVE RANGE: Indo-West Pacific.

MINIMUM AQUARIUM SIZE: 55 gal. (209 L).

OVERVIEW: Green and glorious, this colorful wrasse is a welcome addition to the more passive fish-only tank or reef aquarium. It can be housed in small harems with a single male and several females.

FEEDING: Carnivore. Feed meaty foods such as mysid shrimp and enriched brine shrimp several times a day.

HABBITAT: Reef. This fish needs plenty of swimming room as well as rocky crevices and niches were it can duck into shelter when it feels threatened.

COMPATIBILITY: This fairy wrasse can be housed with a wide variety of tankmates. In larger tanks, it rarely bothers other fishes, with the possible exception of related species (males may pester other fairy wrasses or flasher wrasses). It is more often the victim of harassment by dottybacks, large damsels, hawkfishes, angels, sandperches and triggers. Keep one male per tank. Females can be housed together and with males. Males are more colorful, sporting large areas of red on the head (if from Indian Ocean) or bright red on the fins (if from Pacific). It does not pose a threat to ornamental invertebrates.

AQUARIUM BEHAVIOR: As with others in the genus, it often bobs along as it swims in the water column waiting for zooplankton-like food items to appear. It will perform fabulous displays toward members of its own kind during which the color will intensify. An aquarium top is mandatory to keep this species from leaping out.

FILAMENTED FLASHER WRASSE *Paracheilinus filamentosus*

MAXIMUM LENGTH: 3.9 in. (10 cm).

NATIVE RANGE: West Pacific.

MINIMUM AQUARIUM SIZE: 30 gal. (114 L).

OVERVIEW: One of the most glorious of all the reef fishes, male Filamented Flasher Wrasses engage in a dynamic dance when displaying toward rivals and potential mates. This is a highly commendable fish for peaceful communities and reef aquariums.

FEEDING: Carnivore. Feed meaty foods, at least twice a day.

HABITAT: Reef. Provide swimming space and plenty of hiding places.

COMPATIBILITY: This fish rarely bothers its tankmates, but males may incessantly chase other flasher wrasse species, especially in close quarters. It is often picked on by more aggressive species—if this happens, the flasher will hide most of the time or hang in the upper corners of the aquarium (when stressed like this, the colors become blotchy). Keep one male per tank. You can house a male with one or more females in a more spacious aquarium (over 100 gallons [380L]). Females lack the filaments on the dorsal fin. Flasher wrasses will not harm invertebrates.

AQUARIUM BEHAVIOR: The display of the male is something to behold. The fish will erect all its fins and then dash around the tank like a kite in a strong wind. During this display, the colors also intensify. When it is not trying to impress its tankmates, it will slowly scull about the tank looking for food in the water column and may occasionally pick a morsel off the aquarium bottom. It is prone to leaping from open aquariums.

GOLDEN WRASSE *Halichoeres chrysus*
(Yellow Coris)

MAXIMUM LENGTH: 4.7 in. (12 cm).

NATIVE RANGE: Indo-West Pacific.

MINIMUM AQUARIUM SIZE: 30 gal. (114 L).

OVERVIEW: An under-appreciated, brilliantly garbed wrasse that remains relatively small and readily acclimates to captivity. It can be kept in groups that provide color and interest to a peaceful marine community group.

FEEDING: Carnivore. Feed meaty foods, twice a day.

HABITAT: Reef-sand interface. Provide a sand bed (at least two inches deep) comprised of a finer substrate where it will bury itself at night or when threatened. (Coarse sand may inflict skin injuries.)

COMPATIBILITY: This is normally a very mellow species that rarely, if ever, behaves aggressively toward tankmates. It is more likely to be the target of bullies (namely dottybacks, damselfishes, hawkfishes). You can keep more than one female in the same tank—keep males on their own or with one or more females. (Males have brighter orange bands on their heads and one rather than two spots on the dorsal fin.) This wrasse is not a threat to most ornamental invertebrates with the possible exception of shrimps.

AQUARIUM BEHAVIOR: The Golden Wrasse is a bottom-oriented species that swims about searching the sand or rock surface for edibles. It will follow tankmates that disturb the sand in hopes of pouncing on prey items flushed from hiding by a substrate-disturbing species.

HARLEQUIN TUSKFISH *Choerodon fasciata*

MAXIMUM LENGTH: 9.8 in. (25 cm).

NATIVE RANGE: Indo-Pacific.

MINIMUM AQUARIUM SIZE: 55 gal. (209 L).

OVERVIEW: One of the most distinctive wrasses to make its way into the aquarium world, the Harlequin Tuskfish is an admirable fish, despite its fierce looks and stout blue teeth.

FEEDING: Carnivore. Feed meaty foods such as shrimp, krill, mussels and color-enhancing prepared rations several times a day.

HABITAT: Reef or reef-sand interface. Provide it with plenty of bolt holes and lots of open swimming space.

COMPATIBILITY: While it looks savage, this fish is usually rather mellow. It should not be housed with small fishes, as it has been known to prey on those it can catch. On the positive side, it is usually not aggressive toward unrelated fishes that are not a potential meal. Keep just one per tank as they will often do battle unless the aquarium is very large. It has been known to eat ornamental crustaceans and may be a threat to small snails, clams, and various other invertebrates—its favorite targets in the wild. It will ignore corals, but would otherwise be a poor choice for most reef aquariums.

AQUARIUM BEHAVIOR: While it tends to be initially shy, the Harlequin Tuskfish will become a showy member of the aquarium community. It will swim from crevice to crevice, occasionally stopping to look for prey. If at all possible, attempt to acquire individuals from Australia. They tend to be handled with more care and more readily adapt to life in captivity than those from the Philippines or Indonesia.

LONGFINNED FAIRY WRASSE *Cirrhilabrus rubriventralis*
(Redbellied Fairy Wrasse, Social Wrasse)

MAXIMUM LENGTH: 2.9 in. (7 cm).

NATIVE RANGE: Red Sea and Indian Ocean.

MINIMUM AQUARIUM SIZE: 30 gal. (114 L).

OVERVIEW: This is a beautiful fairy wrasse that engages in a marvelous display where the color intensifies and the fins are spread to increase its apparent size.

FEEDING: Carnivore. Feed meaty foods, preferably several times a day. Color-enhancing rations will help maintain its pigmentation.

HABITAT: Reef or sand-rubble habitat with ample swimming room.

COMPATIBILITY: Females are rarely if ever aggressive toward their neighbors, while males have been known to chase other wrasses, anthias, and dart gobies in smaller tanks. This fish is most likely to be combative with relatives that sport similar colors *(e.g., Cirrhilabrus rubripinnis)*. It is more often attacked by larger, more belligerent fishes (including aggressive damselfishes, hawkfishes and sandperches). Keep one male per tank. Even in large tanks, males may seek each other out and battle. You can keep a male with one or more females (males are red with white belly and have huge pelvic fins, while females are orangish-red with fine blue lines along the body and a dark spot on the caudal peduncle).

AQUARIUM BEHAVIOR: This species spends its day cruising about the tank, often near the substrate, in search of food. It swims in the characteristic fairy wrasse bobbing motion. The aquarium must be covered to prevent jumping.

LUNARE WRASSE *Thalassoma lunare*
(Moon Wrasse)

MAXIMUM LENGTH: 9.8 in. (25 cm).

NATIVE RANGE: Indo-Pacific.

MINIMUM AQUARIUM SIZE: 100 gal. (380 L).

OVERVIEW: This glorious, energetic fish can become a very personable pet while adding color and constant action to a boisterous marine community tank.

FEEDING: Carnivore. Feed meaty foods, at least twice a day. Regular meals of color-enhancing rations will be beneficial.

HABITAT: Reef or reef-sand interface. Provide swimming space and places to hide when the fish is threatened.

COMPATIBILITY: Juveniles usually do not cause problems with other fish species, although they may pick on more diminutive tankmates —especially in a smaller tank. As it grows, a Lunare Wrasse becomes an even greater threat to a variety of fishes. It may even eat smaller or more elongated species. Do not keep it with passive fishes (anthias, chromis, dartfishes, worm gobies). Larger individuals are also a threat to smaller, mild-mannered wrasses. Keep only one per tank. This species will feed on a variety of mobile invertebrates, including small snails, shrimps, crabs, small hermit crabs, serpent stars, small sea stars, and small urchins. It is unsuited to most reef aquariums but will not bother soft or stony corals.

AQUARIUM BEHAVIOR: The Lunare Wrasse is an active species that will spend most of its time swimming around the tank hunting food. This athletic species will jump from an open aquarium.

ORNATE WRASSE *Halichoeres ornatissimus*
(Christmas Wrasse)

MAXIMUM LENGTH: 6.7 in. (17 cm).

NATIVE RANGE: Indo-West Pacific.

MINIMUM AQUARIUM SIZE: 55 gal. (209 L).

OVERVIEW: This much-loved species is ornately adorned with green tattoos on the face, body and fins and readily acclimates to life in the home aquarium that has a sand bed where it can bury itself at night or when it feels threatened.

FEEDING: Carnivore. Feed meaty foods, twice a day.

HABITAT: Reef-sand interface. Provide a sand bed at least two inches deep comprised of a finer coral-sand substrate. Larger, more coarse-grained substrate can lead to injury.

COMPATIBILITY: This species is not overly aggressive toward other fishes, although large males may chase and bully similar wrasses or smaller fishes added to their homes. Keep only one male per tank. Females can be housed together or with a male. While they will not bother corals, larger individuals may attempt to eat ornamental crustaceans.

AQUARIUM BEHAVIOR: This fish will move just over the substrate in search of food. When threatened and at night it will bury under the sand. It may leap from an open aquarium. When first added to the tank, it may take time to adjust to the captive day-night light regimen—they will often bury when it it is night back on the reef where it was collected and come out when it would normally be light on its "home" reef. In time they acclimate to a captive day-night schedule.

REDFIN FAIRY WRASSE *Cirrhilabrus rubripinnis*
(Red Parrot Wrasse, Philippine Flame Wrasse)

MAXIMUM LENGTH: 3.1 in. (8 cm).

NATIVE RANGE: West Pacific.

MINIMUM AQUARIUM SIZE: 30 gal. (114 L).

OVERVIEW: While often overlooked, the Redfin Fairy Wrasse is a striking and interesting aquarium inhabitant. It makes an interesting display when kept in groups with one dominant male and several females.

FEEDING: Carnivore. Feed meaty foods such as mysid shrimp and enriched brine shrimp several times a day.

HABITAT: Reef or sand-rubble habitat. Provide plenty of hiding places, as well as open swimming space.

COMPATIBILITY: This lovely wrasse is rarely troublesome in the community tank. On occasion, males may scrap with other smaller, red fishes (e.g., cardinalfishes), but these squabbles rarely end in injury. It will quarrel with similar fairy wrasses (e.g., *Cirrhilabrus rubriventralis*). This wrasse may be bullied by damselfishes, angelfishes, and hawkfishes. The males, which have a high, sail-like dorsal fin, blue on the throat and longer pelvic fins, should be kept one per tank. They can be housed with one or more females in a larger tank. In cramped quarters, however, they are likely to chase and pester females incessantly.

AQUARIUM BEHAVIOR: This is an active fish that will swim just over the substrate and pick food from the water column. It is a jumper, so keep the aquarium top covered.

SIXLINE WRASSE *Pseudocheilinus hexataenia*

MAXIMUM LENGTH: 3 in. (7.6 cm).

NATIVE RANGE: Indo-West Pacific.

MINIMUM AQUARIUM SIZE: 20 gal. (76 L).

OVERVIEW: This is a diminutive darling that can turn into a demon once it has become established in a smaller tank (that is it may torment smaller, newly introduced tankmates). It is a hardy, interesting fish best kept in larger aquariums with peaceful tankmates.

FEEDING: Carnivore. Feed meaty foods, twice a day. This species will require less frequent feeding in a reef tank with a healthy micro-invertebrate population.

HABITAT: Reef. Provide it with plenty of hiding places. Its natural habitat is often among branching stony corals.

COMPATIBILITY: The Sixline Wrasse can be a good neighbor or a real terror—it depends on the aquarium setting and community. In a larger tank, it rarely bothers its tankmates, but in a smaller tank it can cause real problems. While it can be a troublemaker, it will have a difficult time acclimating if added to a tank containing more boisterous species (e.g., dottybacks, large damselfishes, hawkfishes, pygmy angelfishes). Keep one per tank unless the aquarium is quite large (135 gallons [513 L] or more).

AQUARIUM BEHAVIOR: This fish tends to slink from one hiding place to another, occasionally stopping to survey its domain before disappearing into a nearby crevice or cave. It usually does not bury, but will produce a slime cocoon at night, especially if it is stressed or infested with parasites. It will occasionally "clean" other fishes.

SPANISH HOGFISH *Bodianus rufus*

Mᴀxɪᴍᴜᴍ Lᴇɴɢᴛʜ: 15.7 in. (40 cm).

Nᴀᴛɪᴠᴇ Rᴀɴɢᴇ: Tropical West Atlantic, Caribbean.

Mɪɴɪᴍᴜᴍ Aǫᴜᴀʀɪᴜᴍ Sɪᴢᴇ: 135 gal. (513 L).

Oᴠᴇʀᴠɪᴇᴡ: A common sight on Caribbean reefs, this is a colorful, hardy member of the wrasse family that exhibits interesting behaviors and is a fine choice for larger tanks and robust tankmates.

Fᴇᴇᴅɪɴɢ: Omnivore. Feed meaty and algae-enriched foods at least twice a day. Regular meals of color-enhancing rations will help maintain its bright pigments.

Hᴀʙɪᴛᴀᴛ: Reef or reef-sand interface. Provide plenty of open swimming space as well as some bolt holes it can duck into if threatened.

Cᴏᴍᴘᴀᴛɪʙɪʟɪᴛʏ: The Spanish Hogfish is a peaceful aquarium inhabitant as a juvenile. However, it will fight with members of its own kind or closely related species. As it grows larger, it is capable of eating smaller tankmates and may pick on affable fishes (especially those added after they are already established in their tank home). Keep one per tank, unless your aquarium is huge. It is a dubious selection for the reef tank because of its natural proclivity to dine on a host of invertebrates (including snails, crabs, shrimps, serpent stars, sea stars, urchins). It rarely eats corals, but may knock them over as it looks for food.

Aǫᴜᴀʀɪᴜᴍ Bᴇʜᴀᴠɪᴏʀ: Young Spanish Hogfish act as cleaners and will pick at the fins and body of other fish in the aquarium. They tend to swim about in the water column and just over the substrate, occasionally cocking their head as they search for a meaty morsel.

Red alerts on the big, the bad and the ill-fated

Tales abound in the aquarium trade of naive hobbyists acquiring fishes they thought would be wonderful pets, only to find they have brought home an animal that is either unkeepable or a menace to others. For example, I once had a young woman call me wanting to know what to do with her 4-foot nurse shark that could barely turn around in its 240-gallon (909 L) tank. Bought small, it grew into something she could not handle and that no one (including every public zoo and aquarium for hundreds of miles) would touch.

I have also met many aquarists who purchased coral-feeding butterflyfish only to discover that they could not get them to eat any of the foods available at their local pet store, no matter how hard they tried, coaxed or prayed.

This section is meant to help you avoid these pitfalls. While seasoned aquarists may disagree with my inclusion of one or more species, I can assure you that the track records for all the fishes included here are not acceptable, especially for the greenhorn or casual fishkeeper.

Included here are those that almost always have a difficult time surviving in an aquarium venue. Some—such as the butterflyfish that eat only live coral polyps—have very specialized diets, making it hard to meet their nutritional requirements. Some do not ship well, suffering from excessive stress during their long trip to the wholesaler and aquarium store. Some are very susceptible to disease. Others just outgrow the confines of most aquariums and cannot be expected to live their full life spans in a typical home system.

My ultimate criterion is to ask if there is a significant possibility that a fish of a particular species (or genus) will die prematurely because some special need is impossible or difficult to meet in captivity. If the answer is yes, it qualifies for this list. Whatever the reason, there are some species that are best left on the reef, or that should only be kept by aquarists with the resources and expertise to meet their very specific requirements. As you advance in your aquarium skills and as more information becomes available on their care and feeding, some of these fishes may be worthy of another look.

FLAGFIN ANGELFISH *Apolemichthys trimaculatus*

This angelfish is a bit of an enigma. While others in the genera that have similar sponge-heavy diets do well in the aquarium, this species usually dies from apparent nutritional maladies. Future advances in feeding may change this, but for now it is a fish for experts only.

REASONS TO THINK TWICE:
WHY SOME FISH ARE BEST LEFT IN THE SEA

1. IT WILL BE DIFFICULT OR IMPOSSIBLE TO FEED: Some fish, such as wild seahorses, need several meals of live foods each day. Others, such as the coral-polyp-eating butterflyfishes and sponge-eating angelfishes, have dietary needs that few aquarists could hope to meet.

2. IT GROWS TOO LARGE: Many reef fishes reach adult sizes that require very large tanks or facilities that only public aquariums can provide. Perfect examples are most of the sharks and rays.

3. IT IS NOT LIKELY TO SURVIVE: Certain species, such as the Moorish Idol, have unknown keeping requirements or vulnerability to disease and very seldom adapt successfully to aquarium life.

MULTIBARRED ANGELFISH *(Paracentropyge multifasciata)*

Although strikingly beautiful, this is a delicate species that rarely acclimates to life in the home aquarium. This angelfish is a fastidious, stubbornly finicky feeder that usually hides incessantly until it wastes away from starvation. For advanced aquarists only.

YELLOWSTRIPE ANTHIAS *(Pseudanthias tuka)*

While exceptionally hued and relatively common in the fish trade, this is one of the anthias species that does not tend to fare well in the home aquarium. It often refuses to eat or does not get enough food to thrive. For expert reefkeepers only.

PURPLEMASK ANGELFISH *(Paracentropyge venustus)*

Sadly, this beautiful fish is often reluctant to feed in the home aquarium. Even when it does, it tends to grow progressively thinner and gradually succumbs to starvation. Its diet in the wild is a mystery, and it should be avoided by all but expert fishkeepers.

PINNATE BATFISH *(Platax pinnatus)*

Juveniles are appealing and ornate, but they often refuse food in the home aquarium and are very vulnerable to parasites. They can also attain a large size (17.7 in. [45 cm]), and will outgrow most home tanks. Expert care and a very large, deep aquarium is required.

BENNETT'S BUTTERFLYFISH *(Chaetodon bennetti)*

Known as an obligate corallivore, this is a butterfly genetically pro-
grammed to feed on live coral polyps. It rarely switches to commonly fed aquarium foods, and even if it does, it regularly fades away due
to a lack of needed nutrients.

BLUESPOT BUTTERFLYFISH *(Chaetodon plebeius)*

This is one of the numerous butterflies with a specialized diet that
consists of live corals. It stubbornly ignores even the best aquarium
foods and typically succumbs slowly to a lack of required nutrients.
To be avoided by conscientious aquarists.

EIGHT-BANDED BUTTERFLYFISH *(Chaetodon octofasciatus)*

Although highly appealing, this fish is destined to starve in most aquariums and should be avoided by all but the most advanced aquarists. It is one of many members of the butterflyfish family with a specialized diet demanding a constant supply of live coral polyps.

MEYER'S BUTTERFLYFISH *(Chaetodon meyeri)*

A heartbreaker, this glorious fish needs a daily diet of live coral polyps to survive and is virtually destined to perish in captivity. As with all of the obligate corallivore butterflyfishes, it should be left on the reef unless an expert aquarist can somehow meet its dietary needs.

ORNATE BUTTERFLYFISH *(Chaetodon ornatissimus)*

Unless you have a vast reef tank filled with stony corals ready to be constantly grazed, this gorgeous fish should never be acquired. As with all the coral-eating butterflyfishes, it has an abysmal record of survival in captive systems, even those of professionals.

PACIFIC REDFIN BUTTERFLYFISH *(Chaetodon lunulatus)*

Yet another of the obligate corallivores, this appealing butterfly is almost guaranteed to refuse to eat in captivity. Even if it does pick at some food offerings, it will usually begin a sure terminal decline. Choose one of the hardy, easy-to-keep butterflies instead.

BLACK DAMSEL (Neoglyphidodon melas)

Although a commonly seen fish in the aquarium trade, this is a purchase most hobbyists come to regret. While durable and beautiful when small, it grows large and belligerent enough to take over the entire tank. It turns a drab brown as it grows and will eat soft corals.

GIANT OR JAVANESE MORAY Gymnothorax javanica

This is one of the truly huge moray eels that will outgrow most home aquariums, growing to 9.8 ft. (300 cm) and 66 lbs. (30 kg). There are other marine eels available as cute juveniles that get very large and potentially dangerous. Do your research before buying any moray eel.

RIBBON EEL (*Rhinomuraena quaesita*)

Undeniably appealing, Ribbon Eels are notoriously challenging to feed. Small, live fish (e.g. mollies, guppies) are necessary to entice this eel to feed, if it will eat at all. Note: color variations are tied to age and sex—juveniles are black, males are blue, females are yellow.

BANDED SNAKE EEL (*Myrichthys colubrinus*)

Some fish are best left in the wild, and this is one. Many specimens will never feed in captivity or may need to be fed live fish or live ghost shrimp. It is very shy and needs a deep bed of fine sand where it can escape from view. Best reserved for expert aquarists.

ORANGESPOTTED FILEFISH *(Oxymonacanthus longirostris)*

This is a stunning fish but one that is best avoided because of its specialized diet—it feeds only on small-polyped stony corals. Even those that accept alternate foods usually live a very abbreviated life.

SIGNAL GOBY *(Signigobius biocellatus)*

This beautiful goby species is often sold in pairs. Sadly, they usually starve to death in the home aquarium, not finding enough to eat in the aquarium sand to keep themselves healthy. These fish should be kept only by seasoned aquarists with large, productive reef tanks.

SPECKLED GROUPER *(Epinephelus cyanopodus)*

Here is a greedy eater that will reach large proportions in no time. The juveniles are showy, but they grow large (48 in. [122 cm]), they grow fast, and they grow ugly. Many other groupers fit this same description: always do some research before buying an unknown grouper.

MOORISH IDOL *(Zanclus cornutus)*

While coveted by many aquarists, this elegant fish rarely feeds well in captivity. Some hobbyists have had success keeping it in well-established reef tanks with live rock or feeding live clams, but its specialized dietary needs are hard to replicate in the home aquarium.

BICOLOR PARROTFISH *(Cetoscarus bicolor)*

Parrotfishes generally make poor candidates for the home aquarium, with multiple downsides—they get too large and are too active while seldom getting enough to eat. In the wild, they swim over long distances and feed by scraping algae and polyps from stony corals.

PIPEFISHES *(Syngnathidae)*

Like their close relatives the seahorses, these fishes require live food and often have a difficult time competing with fish tankmates. While some species can be kept in reef tanks with productive refugia, most perish in the home aquarium. Best reserved for experts only.

BLUESPOTTED RIBBONTAIL RAY *(Taeniura lymma)*

Famously beguiling, this beautiful ray can be difficult to feed and will typically perish for unknown reasons. Its track record in home aquariums is dismal. It requires lots of living space (upward of 500 gallons [1894 L])—more than afforded by most home tanks. For experts only.

SEAHORSES *(Syngnathidae)*

Wild-caught seahorses rarely eat anything but live foods, and many seahorse species are endangered, or close to it, overcollected for the Asian folk-medicine trade. Buy only captive-bred specimens, which will be more likely to thrive, and keep them in their own species tank.

NURSE SHARK *(Ginglymostoma cirratum)*

However tempted, please steer clear of this shark. It can easily attain a length of over 10 ft. (3 m). It takes a mammoth system to hold one of these beasts for its entire life. Euthanasia is often the sad end result. Do your research before buying any shark or ray species.

ATLANTIC SPADEFISH *(Chaetodipterus faber)*

Although related to the finicky batfish, this species usually eats voraciously in the home aquarium, getting far too large: 3 ft. (91 cm) and up to 19.8 lb. (9 kg). It is also much too active to squeeze into most home aquariums. Have a large frying pan ready if you buy one.

CLOWN SWEETLIPS *(Plectorhinchus chaetodonoides)*

As endearing as any juvenile fish in the store, these charming little specimens should be avoided. First of all, they often refuse anything but live food and even then rarely eat with gusto. Secondly, those that survive will get very big and need an extra-large aquarium.

SKUNK TILEFISH *(Hoplolatilus marcosi)*

Most of the tilefish in this genus do not readily acclimate to aquarium life. They regularly jump when startled, catapulting themselves out of the tank or against the top of the tank. Feeding is usually difficult. They are best reserved for experienced reef aquarists.

GOLDEN TREVALLY *(Gnathanodon speciosus)*

Also known as Golden Jack, this is a hardy species that is way too active and gets much too large (3.6 ft. [110 cm]) for most home aquariums. The juveniles are colorful, showy tank residents and are often purchased by the uninformed. For really large systems only.

REDTAIL WRASSE *(Anampses chrysocephalus)*

This burying species rarely feeds well in the home aquarium. It will do best in a well-established reef tank with a productive refugium. It also ships poorly and has a poor survival record, even among seasoned fishkeepers. Best left to the determined experts.

HUMPHEAD OR NAPOLEON WRASSE *(Cheilinus undulatus)*

Hunted relentlessly for Asian gourmet food markets, this fish sometimes appears in the aquarium trade. Aside from not buying an endangered fish, you need to know that this species attains the gargantuan size of 7 ft. (2.2 m) in length and over 400 lbs. (191 kg).

HAWAIIAN CLEANER WRASSE *(Labroides phthirophagus)*

Cleaner wrasses, including this species, are all obligatory parasite-pickers and slime-eaters that are virtually guaranteed to starve in the home aquarium. Before wasting away, they may pester fish tankmates by constantly attempting to groom their bodies and fins.

LEOPARD WRASSE *(Macropharyngodon meleagris)*

This and other members of its genus are beautiful wrasses that unfortunately have difficulty getting enough to eat in the home aquarium. They do best in large, well-established reef tanks with live rock and live sand supporting healthy populations of micro-invertebrates.

SMALLTAIL PENCIL WRASSE *(Pseudojuloides cerasinus)*

This and other pencil wrasses are a poor bet for most marine aquarists. They feed only on live microinvertebrates and demand a healthy community of these animals in their home aquarium if they are going to thrive. Best left to the experienced reefkeepers.

How to mix and match fishes in a balanced marine community

Until the recent past, the unique nutritional requirements of captive seawater fishes was often overlooked by hobbyists. People tried to get by using foods meant for freshwater aquarium species, flake foods of terrestrial origin and frozen brine shrimp of questionable quality.

Fortunately, all this is changing. We now know that marine fishes need a diet primarily of marine origin. We recognize that a poor diet can equate to general ill health and greater susceptibility to pathogens. Some commonly observed problems with poorly fed marine fish include lateral line and fin erosion, weight loss, color infidelity, listlessness and disease outbreaks.

The modern day marine fishkeeper now has access to many great foods. One excellent staple is fresh and frozen seafood meant for the family dinner table. Shrimp, clams, squid and marine fish flesh, rinsed and finely chopped are fine foods with the balance of nutrients a marine fish needs.

GRATE YOUR OWN RATIONS

You can take frozen "green" shrimp, squid or marine fish flesh and run it over a cheese grater to produce nice, bite-sized shavings for your fish. Many graters have holes of varying size so you can adjust the size of the shavings to suit the size of the fishes you are feeding. If feeding marine fish flesh, avoid fatty species such as salmon, tuna, and herring, as they will leave an oily film on the water's surface. Also beware that fresh foods can quickly spoil, polluting the aquarium. It is important to remove uneaten pieces from the aquarium bottom and the filter soon after the feeding session. (Better yet, never feed more than your fishes will eat up within five min-

To each its own: Clown Triggerfish displays the distinctive head-standing feeding habit of its family.

utes or less.) Although some writers have suggested that feeding fresh or frozen seafood can spread pathogens to aquarium fish, this is a rare event. Good quality seafoods should pose no greater risk than any other rations.

MARINE AQUARIUM PREPARATIONS

Frozen preparations specially formulated for marine aquarium species offer great convenience and are a wonderful staple food for marine fishes. Some of these are made up specifically for fishes of the various feeding guilds (e.g., carnivore diet, herbivore diet) or even specific taxonomic groups. One manufacturer has a specific formula for angelfishes (which includes sponge fragments), a diet for triggerfishes and also one for small sharks. Most of these frozen preparations consist of a mix of marine proteins (scallop, fish, crustacean flesh), supplemented with pigments, vitamins and essential amino acids. Look for chlorophyll-rich green preparations for herbivores and reddish cubes created for carnivores.

Frozen mysid shrimp are a wonderful "newer" food for marine fishes. Many species that normally can be difficult to feed will accept these succulent little crustaceans with gusto. They are also a nutritious food, relatively high in protein and fats. For example, the combined crude fat and protein content of mysid shrimp is approximately 72 percent, while in brine shrimp it is around 6 percent. Unfortunately, not all frozen mysid shrimp are created equal. Some brands tend to consist of mushy, mysid fragments rather than nice, firm, whole little shrimp.

There is one downside to feeding mysids. They are not high in carotenoids, so if you feed mysids exclusively, certain fish species may exhibit color loss. I recommend supplementing a mysid-heavy diet with some of the frozen preparations or flake foods with added pigments or so-called color enhancers.

Another new and highly nutritious food that is making its way into more and more aquarium stores is Cyclop-eeze®. This

Redbreasted Maori Wrasse shows its ability to attack and swallow large prey items, in this case a live clam. Feeding habits vary from species to species.

is a bright reddish-orange frozen bar composed of a tiny, bio-engineered crustacean from the genus *Cyclops*. This is a food with lots of desirable HUFAs (highly unsaturated fatty acids) and high protein content. It has a very small particle size, it remains in suspension longer, and fish love it. Cyclo-eeze is especially good for small, zooplankton-eating fishes. It drifts around in the water longer than most foods and gives the planktivores time to pick the food particles out of the water column. When feeding this food, be aware that a very small chunk contains a lot of individual *Cyclops*—it is easy to over-feed. A dried form is also available.

COLOR ENHANCERS

Like most aquarists, I do feed some frozen brine shrimp and krill, but would never recommend you use them exclusively. Both of these traditional foods, and many other marine crustaceans, are rich in carotenoid pigments and do help fish retain their bright colors.

In the wild, a French Angelfish is a constant grazer, nipping sponge off hard substrates. In the aquarium, it does best with frequent feedings.

Another way to ensure your fish are getting their nutritional "fix" is to soak fish food in an enhancer such as Selcon®. This contains omega-3 fatty acids and a stabilized form of Vitamin C, vital nutrients that are often missing in aquarium fish diets. It works particularly well if you are feeding freeze-dried foods, like krill, which soak it up like a sponge. When buying frozen brine shrimp, look for the premium, enriched brands.

Flake foods have also come a long way in recent years. There are some wonderful, nutrient-rich flake foods on the market today that are not only good for your fish, but can help maintain their amazing colors. Look for pigment-enhancing rations that will help reduce the likelihood that a spectacular fish will change from dramatic to dull on an ordinary aquarium diet.

Certain flake foods target the nutritional needs of carnivores or herbivores, and new choices are constantly being introduced. Look for the best foods at local aquarium retailers that cater to demanding marine hobbyists.

Pelletized foods and tablet foods vary in their nutritional contents and not all fish are keen to ingest these hardened formulations. With the convenience of dried foods it is easy to offer your fishes more frequent feedings between meals of fresh or frozen rations.

HERBIVORE CHOICES

If you are keeping plant-eating fishes in your home aquarium, you will need to include vegetable matter in their diets. Many aquarists feed their herbivores romaine lettuce, spinach leaves and/or broccoli heads. Freeze or steam the leaf before introducing it into the aquarium to make it easier for the fish to digest these fibrous foods. There are a number of plastic clips with hangers or suction cups on the market that you stick or hang on the inside of the aquarium. This makes it easier for the fish to browse on the vegetable matter. Some aquarists take a piece of coral rubble, attach a leaf to it with a rubber band and drop it to the bottom of the aquarium.

An even better supplement for marine herbivores are the sheets, flakes or chunks of dried macroalgae that are now on the market. Not too long ago, this type of food product was only available to aquarists that had an Asian food market at their disposal. (Nori is dried algae used in the preparation of sushi and now available at many supermarkets.)

Dried algae specifically made for aquarium feeding is now available at many aquarium stores. These products are available in sheets or in chopped up pieces, and they enable the aquarist to feed their herbivores brown, green, and red algae species. You should feed these to your herbivores on a daily basis. Offering a variety of different herbivore foods is the best approach in most cases.

LIVE FOODS

Live foods will be eaten greedily by most aquarium fishes, and they can be used to supplement your fishes' diet or to help induce a fastidious fish to feed. (Those interested in breeding marine fishes know that live foods can be crucial in conditioning broodstock and stimulating spawning behaviors.)

Live brine shrimp and ghost shrimp are a favorite of many marine fishes. It is a good idea to enrich or gut-pack them before feeding them to your fish. Place an enriching supplement such as Selcon, a finely ground, nutritious flake food or Cyclop-eeze in with your live shrimp an hour or more before feeding them to your marine fish.

Freshwater crayfish and fiddler crabs are great treats for predators big enough to take large crustaceans. Freshwater livebearing fish such as mollies and guppies are popular foods but lack the fatty acids that marine fishes need for good health. You can also gut-pack these feeder fish before presenting them to your captive charges, but never rely on them as a regular part of your marine fishes' diet.

Live marine clams or mussels, often available in the seafood section of grocery stores or in fresh fish shops, are a great food. These mollusks are particularly valuable for enticing picky eaters, like certain butterflyfishes and angelfishes, to start feeding. Simply break the shell open with a screw driver and a hammer and then throw the open clam into the tank. The feeding frenzy that ensues is remarkable.

FEEDING FREQUENCY

The amount and frequency of feeding for any particular aquarium will vary to suit the fishes being kept. For our purposes, we can break reef fishes down into three general feeding groups: the herbivores, the carnivores, and the omnivores. (Additionally, zooplanktivores are open-water carnivores.)

Many community tanks have a mix of these different fishes, and the best way to ensure that all their nutritional prerequisites are met is to rely on a varied diet. This means a combination of flake, frozen and fresh foods. Relatively few reef fishes are specialized feeders. For example, the vast majority of carnivores feed on a number of different types of prey, not just a single animal species. With your reef fish, variety is essential to ensure their long-term health.

Poss's Scorpionfish, an ambush predator that eats at random intervals, with a just-caught cleaner shrimp it is about to swallow whole.

The herbivores feed mainly—but not always exclusively—on plant material, and they tend to consume large quantities of food. For example, the Cortez Gregory *(Stegastes rectifraenum)* takes over 3,000 bites in a day's time, and it needs more than 500 bites to fill its gut once. This fish, which reaches a maximum weight of about 2.5 oz (70 gm), consumes about 0.4 oz (11 gm) of algae per day—or approximately 16 percent of its total body weight per day. The human equivalent would be 27 pounds of food for a 170-pound male or 19 pounds for a 120-pound woman.

Herbivores have to consume large quantities of food because algae contains a limited quantity of digestible nutrients and they also have to expend considerable energy in their grazing activities. When keeping herbivores, you should bear these facts in mind, especially if your aquarium is devoid of algae. Rather than giving them one big meal daily, it is best to provide several smaller feedings throughout the day. To supplement this, you can add a piece of dried algae to the aquarium once a day. If your herbivores quickly eat the algae add another— just remember to remove any uneaten pieces after

Zooplanktivores such as these Green Chromis feed constantly during the day, expending considerable energy darting after passing prey items.

12 hours or before you go to bed. I have seen sickly, emaciated tangs become healthy and fat as pregnant cows using this feeding technique.

For anyone keeping a fish-only aquarium, I strongly suggest that you encourage a lush growth of filamentous algae, which will act as a natural food source for these fish. Some of the healthiest captive tang (surgeonfish) I have ever seen have been in tanks with a thick mat of green hair algae on the back glass and rocky substrates. If you have a reef aquarium, or a fish-only tank, the occasional introduction of *Caulerpa* or red macroalgae will be appreciated by browsing fish species.

MEATY MEAL TIMES

Carnivores are the most well-represented fishes on coral reefs. They vary greatly in the types of food they ingest and their hunting techniques. Those groups that feed on encrusting invertebrates (angelfishes, butterflyfishes, filefishes, triggerfishes, puffers and others) are well-known for grazing actively throughout the day. For example, the French Angelfish *(Pomacanthus paru)*, which feeds mainly on sponges in the wild, takes an average of about three bites per minute during daylight hours. Like herbivores, these species need to be fed several small meals during the day rather than one large feast.

Carnivores that hunt small benthic invertebrates also feed often. These species (many dottybacks, cardinalfishes, wrasses, dragonets, gobies) should be fed at least a couple of times per day unless their normal fare is present in appreciable quantities in the tank—usually small crustaceans living and breeding in the live rock or patches of macroalgae.

Larger, predatory fishes—such as morays, lionfishes, and groupers—that feed on bigger prey items usually ingest a sizable prey item once a day. Some even feed less frequently than this (e.g., several times a week).

Zooplankton feeders (anthias, fairy wrasse, flasher wrasses, dartfishes) are well-suited for the home aquarium because of their natural feeding behavior. Aquarists typically introduce food at the water's surface and the fish feed on it as it sinks through the water or as it is blown about the tank by water pumps. This feeding situation is very much like that normally encountered by zooplankton feeders in the wild; that is, they pick moving food out of the water column. It is very important that active zooplanktivores are fed more frequently than most other carnivores. It is best to feed them at least three times a day.

Best Practices for Preventing and Stopping Disease

As marine aquarists, our biggest enemy in maintaining healthy fish is not disease, but stress.

A wild-caught aquarium fish is exposed to stress from the moment the diver unfurls his net and begins trying to catch it. The fish is then transported in a small, unfamiliar environment such as a bucket or live well to holding tanks on shore. In some cases the fish are handled carefully and provided with proper care in the coming days or even weeks, but not always. From collection stations and exporters in the tropics, through wholesale facilities in the importing countries, the fish are usually held in bare tanks. This makes it easier for staff or customers to observe the fish and maintain clean conditions.

But, think about this from the fish's perspective. You have been living in an environment without walls, feeling reasonably safe and secure within or near a protective coral labyrinth, where hiding places abound. Now the world is a little clear-sided box without privacy or shelter. Even if other environmental parameters such as temperature and water quality are optimal, a coral reef fish is more than likely going to experience some degree of stress. Realistically, during the process of getting from the reef to your local retailer, marine fishes are exposed to exercise stress, suboptimal water quality and high levels of ammonia, temperature fluctuations and lack of proper nutrition.

STRESS FACTORS

True, stresses can kill some fish outright, but the effects are not always so dramatic or so immediate. Studies have shown that stress can cause short and long-term physiological changes. It can trigger hormonal changes, upset respiration, cause osmoregulatory and metabolic disturbances, elevate blood sugar levels, and other more subtle upsets. Some fish rebound from these stressful encounters, while others may die

Schooling Bannerfish: the move from reef to aquarium can lead to disease.

days or even weeks after the initial shock. Stress factors also cause immune suppression, which can open the way for the parasitic and bacterial infections that marine aquarists have learned to regard with trepidation and concern.

In order to keep your fish healthy, it is essential to try to provide them with a stress-free environment as soon as they arrive in our home aquariums. A good marine fish retailer will have started the process, but the major responsibility falls to the home aquarist.

There is no doubt that different species of reef fishes can withstand different levels of stress. This may be one of the more important determining factors when considering how well a species does in your home aquarium. Not only are there species-specific differences in the ability to withstand stress, there can be noteworthy differences between size classes. For example, *Pomacanthus* angelfishes between 2 and 4 inches tend to ship better and acclimate more readily to captivity than either tiny juveniles or large adults. In general, healthy young fish survive capture and transport and the acclimation to captivity better than large adult specimens.

All these factors need to be taken into consideration when selecting fish for your home aquarium. In this book, we have tried to make this process easier by only including species that tend to be more stress-resistant—but that is not to say these fish will not succumb to stress-related maladies as well.

QUARANTINE: YOUR BEST TOOL

The best way to ensure that a fish is healthy before placing it into your display aquarium is to quarantine it in a small isolation tank. Quarantine is the near-surefire way to let a new fish recover from shipping stress and to be sure it is not bringing a world of woes and disease-causing pathogens into your display aquarium.

I have had numerous people tell me that they could never afford a quarantine tank, only to hear later that they ended up losing a whole tank of fish worth much more than any quarantine set-up to a virulent parasite. In my mind a quarantine tank is as important to successful marine fishkeeping as a hydrom-

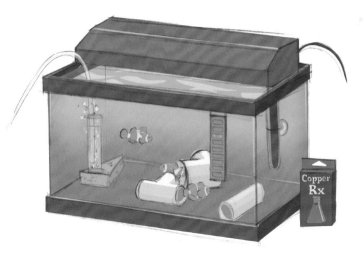

A quarantine tank can double as a hospital tank where sick fish can be treated without introducing potent medications into the display aquarium.

eter. By quarantining your fish you will have the opportunity to observe—and medicate them appropriately, if need be—before they are introduced to the display aquarium.

All you need is a 10-gallon (38 L) tank, a light, a heater, a thermometer, an air pump, an airstone and some saltwater. If you are quarantining larger, more active fish species then you may need a 30-gallon (114 L) tank. You can use a sponge filter or small power filter filled with a plastic filter media (no crushed coral or carbon should be placed in these filters) for biological filtration. The filter can be "seeded" with beneficial bacteria from an established display aquarium by squeezing some water from a working filter sponge or pad and circulating it through the quarantine tank water and filter.

If you use a filter, it is essential that you sterilize the filter and filter media after the quarantine period is completed and before using it again. To do this, soak all the filter parts in a mild chlorine solution (2% chlorine, the rest tap water) for 24 to 48 hours and then rinse it repeatedly with fresh water until the chlorine smell is gone. To ensure all the chlorine has been reduced, soak the filter components in a bucket of fresh water to which chlorine remover has been added. Rinse again.

If not using an established biological filter, you can just add an air stone and do frequent water exchanges (every third day change about 10-15% of the water) to prevent the build-up of nitrogenous waste products. Although you need to be sure your fish is properly fed during the quarantine period, it is important not to overfeed. Remove any uneaten food from the aquarium immediately.

A couple of hiding caves will be appreciated by many fish while in quarantine. Sections of white PVC pipe, plastic PVC fittings or weighted plastic flower pots are perfect temporary shelters and can be sterilized between uses.

I recommend keeping a new fish in quarantine for at least three weeks. (Public aquariums with priceless collections of fish often wait a full month before putting a new specimen on display.) It is important to observe the fish frequently and closely during this period and to promptly treat them if a problem arises. If treatment is necessary, be sure to leave the fish in quarantine at least 10 days after the full course of the treatment is completed to ensure that they have fully recovered.

One important rule when quarantining is that a fish must go through the entire three week process without being exposed to any other fish. If a new fish is added to the quarantine tank while another specimen is still being isolated, you must start the whole three week process over again.

WHEN DISEASE HAPPENS

Captive coral reef fishes are susceptible to a number of different parasites. These typically appear as consequences of stress—when fishes are shipped, subjected to sudden temperature shifts or when water conditions deteriorate.

In order to deal with these potentially lethal infestations, it is important to be able to diagnosis which parasite is present. With the use of quarantine and good husbandry practices, most hobbyists won't have to become underwater veterinarians, but from time to time we must administer drugs and apply various treatment regimens to save our fish.

If a fish does show signs of disease in your display aquarium, act immediately. There is truth in this old saying: "He who hesitates has dead fish." I know I've ignored the initial signs of a parasitic infection in hopes that the potentially ill fish would

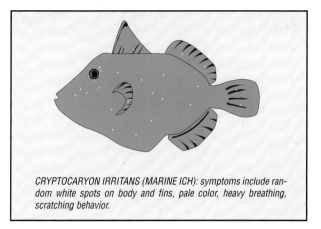

CRYPTOCARYON IRRITANS (MARINE ICH): symptoms include random white spots on body and fins, pale color, heavy breathing, scratching behavior.

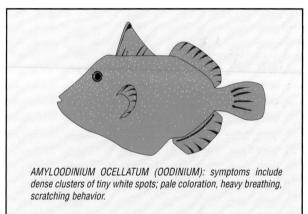

AMYLOODINIUM OCELLATUM (OODINIUM): symptoms include dense clusters of tiny white spots; pale coloration, heavy breathing, scratching behavior.

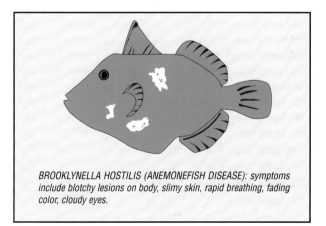

BROOKLYNELLA HOSTILIS (ANEMONEFISH DISEASE): symptoms include blotchy lesions on body, slimy skin, rapid breathing, fading color, cloudy eyes.

EXTERNAL PARASITES AND TREATMENT

Species	Symptoms	Treatment	Remarks
Coral Fish Disease, Velvet Disease (Amyloodinium ocellatum)	Very small white spots that look like dust on body surface and fins; pale coloration, heavy respiration, scratching on substrate.	0.2 mg/l Cu^{2+} for up to three weeks; freshwater dip; formalin bath (1 ml/ gallon for one hour); benzalkonium chloride bath (1 mg/L for one hour, repeat in 24 hours).	Dinoflagellate. Very virulent.
Marine Ich, Whitespot (Cryptocaryon irritans)	Small white spots on body surface and fins; pale coloration, heavy breathing, scratching on substrate.	Formalin bath (as above); reduce salinity (drop to 13% – or a specific gravity of 1.010 - for 7 to 10 days); combination of Quinine Hydrochloride (3.96 mg/L) and Chloroquine (15.90 mg/L); freshwater dip.	Ciliate protozoan. Common but often easy to treat.
Uronema Disease (Uronema marinum)	Lesions, sloughing of slime and skin, lethargy.	Formalin and malachite green medications; freshwater dips.	Ciliate protozoan. Very virulent.
Clownfish Disease (Brooklynella hostilis)	Heavy respiration, excessive slime production, body lesions, color fades, cloudy eyes.	Formalin and malachite green medications.	Ciliate protozoan.
Black Ich, Yellow Tang Disease (Paravortex sp.)	Small black spots on the body surface, particularly visible on light colored fishes, loss of color, scratching on substrate, loss of appetite.	Freshwater dip; formalin bath (as above); Praziquantel bath (20 mg/L for 3 hours); cleaner species; reduction of salinity (drop to 15 % – or a specific gravity of 1.012 – for 7 to 10 days).	Turbellarian worm. Most commonly observed on surgeon and rabbitfishes, but infects other families as well.
Flukes	Scratching on substrate, color loss, increased respiration, lack of appetite; may show-up as small, opaque shapes on body surface.	Freshwater dip; formalin medications; trichlorfon bath (0.15 mg/L); Praziquantel bath (10 mg/L for 3 hours); cleaner species.	Monogenetic trematodes. Often misdiagnosed. Fish often die due to secondary bacterial infections.
Copepods and Isopods	Small crustaceans that are visible with the naked eye on the body, fins or eyes. Also infest gills.	Freshwater dip; formalin medications; trichlorfon bath (0.15 mg/L); Praziquantel bath (10 mg/L for 3 hours); cleaner species.	Crustacean parasites. Not commonly observed on aquarium fishes.

somehow shake off the problem on its own only to have the original carrier as well as every other fish in the tank break out in a full-blown and ultimately fatal infestation. Newcomers to marine fishkeeping are often astonished at how lethal some of the parasitic infections can be.

Prompt treatment will often mean the difference between recuperation and catastrophe. The longer you wait to remove a fish showing signs of a parasitic infection from your display tank and commence the prescribed treatment regimen, the more likely that fish will die and other fish in the tank will be infected with the same parasite (if they are not already manifesting symptoms).

This is especially true in the case of virulent parasites like *Amyloodinium* or *Uronema*. By immediately removing an infected specimen you may be able to prevent the whole fish population from contracting the same disease or parasite. If most of the fish in your tank are falling prey to the parasite, it's best to treat the fish in the display aquarium—unless, of course, it's a reef aquarium. If you have a reef aquarium, always have an effective fish trap ready in case you need to rapidly remove a sick fish. Or, be ready to tear the tank apart if intervention is necessary.

FISHY FIRST AID KIT

One way to ensure that you can act promptly when a sick fish is detected is to have a hospital tank and the necessary medications waiting in the wings. Again, here is a time when a quarantine tank can prove to be worth its weight in gold. It may be 24 hours from the time you first recognize symptoms of an illness and have access to medications at your local store. I like to have a fishy first aid kit on hand. I would include some formalin (be careful, this chemical is carcinogenic, poisonous and flammable), some non-chelated copper, a copper test kit, some Nitrofurazone, and a pH test kit with sodium bicarbonate to raise pH if a freshwater dip is needed. Be aware that many medicines have a limited shelf life. Check the expiration dates on the drug containers once in a while to be sure that they haven't lost their efficacy.

Familiarize yourself with the more common marine fish diseases and parasites. (See Chart on page 176 for symptoms and treatments.) I recommend picking up one or more good marine-fish reference books so that you can familiarize yourself with the various pathogens and treatment regimens. Two of my favorites are Moe (1992) and Bassler (1996).

BE WATCHFUL

Perhaps the most important habit of successful marine fish-keepers is taking at least a few minutes each day just to observe their charges and do a quick check of all systems. In today's busy world, some people set up a tank, only to give it as much attention as a smoke alarm. If you don't have time to give some daily attention to your aquarium, you shouldn't keep saltwater fish (or if you do, be sure you purchase only those species with "bulletproof" constitutions).

With most marine fish community tanks, there is a strong correlation between the amount of time you invest in them and your level of success. I am not just talking about time spent on feeding and routine maintenance. It is also important that you sit quietly in front of the tank and observe your fish and their captive environment. Not only is it the best part of keeping marine fishes, it also enables you to learn about how the fish should behave and notice when the fish are behaving abnormally.

For example, a watchful aquarist will notice when a fish is respiring more heavily than normal, when one fish is starting to pick on a subordinate tankmate, or when the eyes of a fish begin to look opaque. These observations will enable you to respond to a potential problem in a timely manner. If you never watch your fish, you wouldn't be aware of the fish's normal respiratory rate, nor will you know why a fish is suddenly spending all its time in the upper corner of the tank.

In my many years in the hobby I have known many aquarists who are more interested in the chemistry and gadgetry involved in the hobby than with the organisms they maintain. They can tell you exactly what their calcium and phosphate levels are, how much water their pump can deliver at 3, 6 or 8

Copper Controversy & Two Alternatives

Copper-based medications are recommended for several common marine parasites, but some experts have started to argue that these medications often do more harm than good. Copper is not always effective in treating these parasites, and maintaining the proper therapeutic copper levels in the aquarium witout overdosing is often hard to do. Exposure to this heavy metal can be very stressful to the patient, suppressing its natural immune response. Copper is deadly to most reef invertebrates, and, at high enough levels, it is also poisonous to fish. Among the fishes most-sensitive to copper treatments are the elasmobranchs (sharks and rays) and seahorses, as well as jawfishes, mandarinfishes and, according to some reports, certain pygmy angelfishes.

If a display tank has ever been treated with copper, some of the copper ions may still be bound to the substrate and filtration media, and if the pH drops in such a system, the copper will be released from the substrate back into solution. A drop of less than 0.2 pH points can cause enough copper to be released to cause a problem for more sensitive species. Rather than using copper-based medications, alternative treatment methods can be tried.

Some hobbyists swear by garlic-oil-laced foods, although this treatment may still be in the realm of folk medicine. Another more scientific approach is to lower the specific gravity in your hospital or quarantine tank to 1.010-1.011 for 10 to 14 days. (Called the Hyposalinity Treatment, it can also be used in the display tank if sensitive invertebrates are not present.) This tactic is designed to cause osmotic shock to the parasites, forcing them to burst. You should drop the specific gravity over a period of several hours. When returning the tank to normal salinity (1.020-1.025), do so over a period of two to three days.

feet of head, and how many bubbles travel-up their skimmer in a minute's time, but they can't tell you what species of fish or invertebrates they have, what they eat in the wild, what habitat they normally live in or what part of the world they come from. Knowing something about an animal's natural history and behavior is just as important as knowing your water parameters and equipment specs. If you understand the animals you keep and develop an ability to read their behaviors, you can use them as living indicators of the tank's condition.

The smart marine aquarist always has some clean seawater mixed and ready to go. I recommend having at least one 30-gallon (114 L) trash can (used only for this purpose) with premixed seawater. (If you have a smaller tank and fewer fish you may get away with a smaller water reservoir.) I like to keep a small powerhead and heater suspended in the reservoir (keep the heater off the bottom) so that the water is warm, well mixed and ready for immediate use if problems arise. An emergency water supply can come in handy if your aquarium water deteriorates quickly—for example, if you have a larger fish or invertebrate die and decompose in your tank, if you have to do a quick water change or if the tank should start to leak.

FRESHWATER DIPS

The freshwater bath can be helpful in eradicating some marine fish parasites. It works by exposing single-celled parasites to a markedly different salinity. The osmotic gradient that exists between the parasites' internal environment and its surroundings results in water diffusing into their bodies. This causes some parasites to burst like an overfilled balloon.

Unfortunately, the freshwater bath is not one hundred percent effective at eliminating all the parasites on a fish. For example, those parasites that are deeply imbedded in the fish's mucus, skin or gills will be unaffected by the bath. Some parasites, like saltwater ich *(Cryptocaryon irritans)* and coral reef disease *(Amyloodinium ocellatum)*, may enter their host's internal

---

WAYS TO REDUCE STRESS IN THE AQUARIUM

- SELECT THE SPECIES you keep carefully—not all species deal with stress in the same way.
- FEED YOUR FISH a nutritious diet.
- SELECT TANKMATES carefully to help avoid aggression problems.
- PROVIDE PLENTY of hiding places.
- MAINTAIN OPTIMAL environmental conditions (good water quality, steady temperature, regular lighting cycles).
- REDUCE THE LIKELIHOOD of sudden changes in environmental conditions.
- CAPTURING, MOVING OR HANDLING your fish should be done as little as possible.

Helfrich's Firefish with telltale clamped fins and early signs of marine ich (Cryptocaryon irritans), seen as scattered white dots on the body and fins.

organs as well, and are thus unaffected by a freshwater bath. Studies have shown that *Cryptocaryon* cysts, which are known as trophonts, can withstand short-term exposure to low salinities. In fact, they can survive in freshwater for up to 18 hours. Other parasites, though not destroyed when a fish is immersed in freshwater, will drop free of their hosts. For example, those *Amyloodinium* cysts not deep in their host's mucus are dislodged when a fish is placed in freshwater.

To administer a freshwater bath, place the fish in a bucket (which is designated for aquarium use only) that contains reverse osmosis water that is the same temperature and pH as the fish's aquarium water. Leave the fish in the bucket for two to eight minutes, but watch it carefully and remove it and place it in the tank if it seems extremely distressed. Warning signs are swimming about the bucket erratically, laying on its side, or attempting to jump out of the bucket. Some species are more sensitive to being exposed to a freshwater bath than others. For example, certain wrasses and mandarinfish or dragonets should not be dipped. The freshwater in the bucket may contain parasites that have dropped off, so try not to transfer water from the bucket into the tank. The best way to avoid this is to quickly lift the fish out of the bucket and into the aquarium with a soft fish net.

✠ **PROBLEM: FISH DOES NOT EAT**

PROBABLE CAUSES: 1. Being picked on by one or more tankmates. 2. Inappropriate foods. 3. Poor water quality.

SOLUTIONS: 1. Closely observe behavior of fishes and if being picked on, remove aggressor or recipient of aggression 2. Try a different food or a live food. Use a vitamin B12 supplement added to water to increase appetite. 3. Do water tests. If needed, try a series of 20% water changes and add fresh activated carbon to filtration.

✠ **PROBLEM: FISH BREATHING MORE HEAVILY THAN NORMAL**

PROBABLE CAUSES: 1. Water temperature too high. 2. Low oxygen level in water. 3. Chemical poisoning. 4. Bullying. 5. Parasites.

SOLUTIONS: 1. Check water temp and make sure heater is not malfunctioning; if heater is working, turn up air-conditioning, acquire a chiller or think about moving tank to a cooler part of the house. 2. Make sure the power is on and pumps are functioning. 3. If poisoning is suspected, move the fish out of the tank to clean water as quickly as possible. 4. Remove the bully or fish being bullied or try rearranging tank to disrupt territorial boundaries. 5. Treat for parasites (page 176).

✠ **PROBLEM: FISH COWERS IN UPPER CORNER OR CONSTANTLY HIDES**

PROBABLE CAUSES: 1. Fish is being picked on by tankmates. 2. Fish is naturally secretive or nocturnal.

SOLUTIONS: 1. Observe behavior of fishes for extended period and, if necessary, remove aggressor or recipient of aggression. 2. Be sure proper hiding places provided for fish that instinctively tend to hide. Add live rock caves, overhangs and sheltering "bolt holes."

✠ **PROBLEM: FISH HAS FRAYED OR TORN FINS.**

PROBABLE CAUSES: 1. Tankmate is nipping at its fins. 2. Fin rot (bacterial infection).

SOLUTIONS: 1. Identify and remove nipping fish species. 2. Treat with antibiotics in separate hospital tank.

✠ **PROBLEM: FISH HAS WHITE SPOTS LIKE PIMPLES**

PROBABLE CAUSE: Marine Ich (*Cryptocaryon irritans*).

SOLUTIONS: Remove infected fish immediately and treat in hospital tank (page 176).

✠ **PROBLEM: FISH LOOKS AS IF IT HAS BEEN ROLLED IN SUGAR**

PROBABLE CAUSE: Coral Fish Disease (*Amyloodinium ocellatum*)

SOLUTION: Remove infected fish immediately and treat in hospital tank (page 176).

✠ **PROBLEM: FISH HAS BLACK SPOTS ON BODY**

PROBABLE CAUSE: Black Ich from Turbellarian flatworms.

SOLUTION: Remove infected fish immediately and treat in hospital tank (page 176).

✠ **PROBLEM: SKIN ALONG LATERAL LINE AND HEAD PORES TURNS PALE**

PROBABLE CAUSE: Head and Lateral Line Erosion (HLLE), a malady most often seen in tangs and angelfishes.

Male Cooper's Anthias displaying aggressive posture. A bullying fish or its constant victim may need to be removed if harassment is serious.

SOLUTIONS: 1. Feed a diet rich in Vitamin A such as heads of broccoli (will only be eaten by herbivores) or add vitamin supplements to food. 2. Stop using carbon in filtration or add a protein skimmer. (One theory is that carbon particles can clog the pores of the lateral line. Skimming may help remove them.)

✠ PROBLEM: FISH DISAPPEARS

PROBABLE CAUSES: 1. Fish has jumped out of tank. 2. Fish is in filter/sump. 3. Fish has died in hidden place. 4. Consumed by tankmates.

SOLUTIONS: 1. Be sure aquarium is properly covered in future. 2. Check filter/sump and extract fish. Add better overflow protection to keep fishes out. 3. If missing specimen is large, try to find and remove corpse. Do water change if water smells foul or is cloudy.. 4. Regard large predators (fish, anemones, brittle stars, crabs, lobsters) with suspicion.

✠ PROBLEM: SUDDEN FISH DEATH

PROBABLE CAUSES: 1. Water too hot, too cold or lacking oxygen. 2. Chemical poisoning. 3. Hydrogen sulfide poisoning from disturbing deep sand bed or from turning on canister filter that has been left off and not opened and cleaned 4. Toxic tank syndrome. 5. Fish aggression. 6. Disease.

SOLUTIONS: 1. Check temperature, heater, pumps. Take immediate corrective action if needed. 2. If poisoning is suspected, do a 50% water change or move the fish out of the tank to clean water as quickly as possible. (Glass cleaners are highly toxic. Use only aquarium-safe, dedicated tools, sponges, etc. in and around the aquarium.) 3. Do not disturb deep sand beds; if this happens, do a 75% water change. 4. If all or most fish die, tear tank down and start again with a good protein skimmer to prevent build-up of toxins. 5. If one fish has killed another, consider removing the aggressor. 6. If all fish die due to disease or parasites, do a large (50% or more) water change, remove sand from aquarium, raise temperature to 86°F (30°C), wait four weeks, reduce temperature and begin adding fish slowly.

[Species to avoid in red]

Amblyeleotris
  fasciata, 29, 30, 99
  latifasciata, 100
Amphiprion
  clarkii, 36, 70
  frenatus, 35, 73
  ocellaris, 32, 33, 72
Anampses
  chrysocephalus, 157
Apogon
  cyanosoma, 31, 32, 69
Apolemichthys
  trimaculatus, 143
  xanthurus, 36, 45
Assessor
  flavissimus, 29, 31, 55
Bodianus
  rufus, 141
Calloplesiops
  altivelis, 74
Centropyge
  argi, 41
  bispinosa, 35, 42
  flavicauda, 49
  vrolikii, 35, 44
Cephalopholis
  miniata, 36, 106
Cetoscarus
  bicolor, 153
Chaetodipterus
  faber, 155
Chaetodon
  auriga, 36, 61
  bennetti, 146
  kleinii, 63
  lunulatus, 148
  meyeri, 147
  miliaris, 64

  octofasciatus, 147
  ornatissimus, 148
  plebeius, 146
  ulietensis, 33, 62
Cheilinus
  undulatus, 158
Choerodon
  fasciatus, 35, 135
Chromis
  cyanea, 32, 76
  viridis, 37, 78
Chrysiptera
  cyanea, 77
  parasema, 33, 83
  talboti, 82
Cirrhilabrus
  cyanopleura, 129
  exquisitus, 132
  rubripinnis, 34, 139
  rubriventralis, 37, 136
Cirrhitichthys
  falco, 31, 109
Congrogadus
  subducens, 33, 86
Cryptocentrus
  cinctus, 33, 102
  leptocephalus, 98
Cyprinocirrhites
  polyactis, 33, 111
Dascyllus
  aruanus, 81
  trimaculatus, 79
Dendrochirus
  zebra, 33, 114
Diodon
  holocanthus, 116
Echidna
  nebulosa, 33, 115

Ecsenius
    bicolor, 34, 56
    midas, 32, 37, 58
    stigmatura, 31, 60
Elacatinus
    oceanops, 29, 97
Emblemaria
    diphyodontis, 30, 59
Epinephelus
    cyanopodus, 152
Forcipiger
    flavissimus, 32, 34, 66
Genicanthus
    lamarck, 47
Ginglymostoma
    cirratum, 155
Gnathanodon
    speciosus, 157
Gobiodon
    okinawae, 30, 101
Gomphosus
    varius, 36, 128
Gramma
    loreto, 29, 31, 32, 103
Grammistes
    sexlineatus, 119
Gymnothorax
    javanica, 149
Halichoeres
    chrysus, 31, 134
    ornatissimus, 33, 138
Heniochus
    acuminatus, 34, 65
Holacanthus
    ciliaris, 36, 48
Hoplolatilus
    marcosi, 156

Hypoplectrus
    gemma, 104
Labroides
    phthirophagus, 158
Liopropoma
    rubre, 32, 107
Macropharyngodon
    meleagris, 159
Meiacanthus
    oualauensis, 30, 57
Melichthys
    vidua, 36, 126
Myrichthys
    colubrinus, 150
Nemateleotris
    decora, 29, 30, 95
    magnifica, 29, 30, 94
Neoglyphidodon
    melas, 149
Odonus
    niger, 35, 36, 124
Opistognathus
    aurifrons, 29, 32, 112
Oxycirrhites
    typus, 34, 110
Oxymonacanthus
    longirostris, 151
Paracentropyge
    multifasciata, 144
    venustus, 145
Paracheilinus
    filamentosus, 133
Paracirrhites
    arcatus, 35, 108
Parapercis
    schauinslandii, 118
Pervagor
    spilosoma, 93

Pholidichthys
 leucotaenia, 75
Pictichromis
 diadema, 87
 porphyrea, 88
Platax
 pinnatus, 145
Plectorhinchus
 chaetodonoides, 156
Plectranthias
 inermis, 30, 32, 54
Pomacanthus
 maculosus, 36, 37, 50
 paru, 43
 semicirculatus, 46
Pomacentrus
 auriventris, 80
Premnas
 biaculeatus, 36, 71
Pseudanthias
 bartlettorum, 34, 51
 rubrizonatus, 53
 squamipinnis, 37, 52
 tuka, 144
Pseudocheilinus
 hexataenia, 34, 140
 octotaenia, 131
Pseudochromis
 aldabraensis, 29, 36, 89
 flavivertex, 92
 fridmani, 37, 90
 springeri, 37, 91
Pseudojuloides
 cerasinus, 159
Pterapogon
 kauderni, 67

Ptereleotris
 evides, 84
 zebra, 33, 85
Pterois
 volitans, 33, 113
Rhinecanthus
 aculeatus, 31, 125
Rhinomuraena
 quaesita, 150
Serranus
 tortugarum, 32, 105
Siganus
 vulpinus, 36, 117
Signigobius
 biocellatus, 151
Sphaeramia
 nematoptera, 31, 34, 68
Stonogobiops
 nematodes, 29, 30, 96
Sufflamen
 bursa, 127
Syngnathidae, 153, 154
Taeniura
 lymma, 154
Thalassoma
 bifasciatum, 130
 lunare, 137
Xanthichthys
 auromarginatus, 33, 123
Zanclus
 cornutus, 152
Zebrasoma
 flavescens, 36, 122
 veliferum, 35, 121
 xanthurum, 36, 37, 120

Recommended References

Bassler, G. 1996. Diseases in Marine Aquarium Fish. Bassler Biofish, Belgium, 96 pp.

Blasiola, G. C. Diseases of Ornamental Marine Fishes. In: Aquariology: The Science of Fish Health and Management. Tetra Sales, Morris Plains, NJ, 275-300 pp.

Bower, C. E. 1983. The Basic Marine Aquarium. Charles C. Thomas Pub. Springfield, Ill. 269 pp.

Garratt, D., T. Hayes, T. Lougher and D. Mills. 2005. 500 Ways to be a Better Marine Aquarist. Interpet Pub., Dorking, Surrey, 128 pp.

Hemdal, J.F. 2006. Advanced Marine Aquarium Techniques. T.F.H. Pub., Neptune City, NJ, 352 pp.

Michael, S. 2001. Marine Fishes. Microcosm/T.F.H. Pub., Neptune City, NJ, 448 pp.

 - 2005. Reef Aquarium Fishes. Microcosm/T.F.H. Pub., Neptune City, NJ, 448 pp.

Moe, M.A. 1992. The Marine Aquarium Handbook: Beginner to Breeder. Green Turtle Pub., Plantation, FL. 318 pp.

Nilsen, A. J. and S. A. Fosså. 2002. Reef Secrets. T.F.H. Pub. Neptune City, NJ, 240 pp.

Spotte, S. Captive Seawater Fishes; Science and technology. John Wiley and Sons, Inc. New York, 942 pp

Wittenrich, M.L. 2007. The Complete Illustrated Breeder's Guide to Marine Aquarium Fishes. Microcosm/T.F.H. Pub., Neptune City, NJ, 304 pp.

COMMON NAME INDEX

[Species to avoid in red]

ANGELFISHES
Cherub, 35, 41
Coral Beauty, 35, 42
Flagfin, 143
French, 43
Halfblack, 35, 44
Indian Yellowtail, 36, 45
Koran, 46
Lamarck's, 47
Multibarred, 144
Purplemask, 145
Queen, 36, 48
Whitetail Pygmy, 49
Yellowbar, 36, 37, 50

ANTHIAS
Bartlett's, 34, 51
Lyretail, 37, 52
Redbar, 53
Unarmed Perchlet, 30, 32, 54
Yellowstripe, 144

ASSESSORS & COMETS
Comet, 74
Yellow Assessor, 29, 31, 55

BATFISHES: Pinnate, 145

BLENNIES
Bicolor, 34, 56
Canary Fang, 30, 57
Midas, 32, 37, 58
Sailfin, 30, 59
Tailspot, 31, 60

BUTTERFLYFISHES
Auriga, 36, 61
Bennett's, 146
Bluespot, 146
Doublesaddle, 33, 62
Eightbanded, 147
Klein's, 36, 63
Lemon, 64

Longfin Bannerfish, 34, 65
Longnose, 32, 34, 66
Meyer's, 147
Ornate, 148
Pacific Redfin, 148

CARDINALFISHES
Banggai, 67
Pajama, 31, 34, 68
Yellowstriped, 31, 32, 69

CLOWNFISHES
Clark's, 36, 70
Maroon, 36, 71
Ocellaris, 32, 33, 72
Tomato, 35, 73

CONVICT BLENNY, 75

COMET, 74

DAMSELFISHES
Black, 149
Blue Chromis, 32, 76
Blue Devil, 77
Bluegreen Chromis, 37, 78
Domino, 79
Goldbelly, 80
Humbug Dascyllus, 81
Talbot's Demoiselle, 82
Yellowtail, 33, 83

DARTFISHES
Scissortail, 84
Zebra, 33, 85

DOTTYBACKS
Carpet Eel Blenny, 33, 86
Diadem, 87
Magenta, 88
Neon, 29, 36, 89
Orchid, 37, 90
Springer's, 37, 91
Sunrise, 92

EELS:
Banded Snake, 150
Giant or Javanese Moray,149
Ribbon, 150
Snowflake Moray, 33, 115
FILEFISHES
Fantail, 93
Orangespotted, 151
FIREFISHES
Firefish, 29, 30, 94
Purple, 29, 30, 95
GOBIES
Blackray Shrimp, 29, 30, 96
Neon Goby, 29, 97
Pinkspotted Shrimp, 98
Redbanded Shrimp, 29, 30, 99
Signal Goby, 151
Spottail Shrimp Goby, 100
Yellow Clown Goby, 30, 101
Yellow Shrimp Goby, 33, 102
GOLDEN TREVALLY, 157
GRAMMA: Royal, 29, 31, 32, 103
GROUPERS AND SEA BASS
Blue Hamlet, 104
Chalk Bass, 32, 105
Coral Hind, 36, 106
Speckled Grouper, 152
Swissguard Basslet, 32, 107
HAWKFISHES
Arc-eye, 35, 108
Falco's, 31, 109
Longnose, 34, 110
Lyretail, 33, 111
JAWFISHES: Yellowhead, 29, 32, 112
LIONFISHES
Common, 33, 113
Zebra, 33, 114
MOORISH IDOL, 152
MORAY EEL: Snowflake, 33, 115
PARROTFISHES: Bicolor, 153
PIPEFISHES, 153

PORCUPINEFISHES: Spiny Puffer, 116
RABBITFISHES: Foxface, 36, 117
RAY: Bluespotted Ribbontail,154
SANDPERCHES: Redspotted, 118
SEAHORSES, 154
SHARKS: Nurse, 155
SOAPFISHES: Six-striped, 119
SPADEFISHES: Atlantic, 155
SWEETLIPS: Clown, 156
TANGS
Purple, 36, 37, 120
Sailfin, 35, 121
Yellow, 36, 122
TILEFISHES: Skunk, 156
TRIGGERFISHES
Bluechin, 33, 123
Niger, 35, 36, 124
Picasso, 31, 125
Pinktail, 36, 126
Scimitar, 127
WRASSES
Bird, 36, 128
Bluehead Fairy, 129
Bluehead, 130
Eightline, 131
Exquisite Fairy, 132
Filamented Flasher, 133
Golden, 31, 134
Harlequin Tuskfish, 35, 135
Hawaiian Cleaner, 158
Humphead or Napolean, 158
Leopard, 159
Longfinned Fairy, 37, 136
Lunare, 137
Ornate, 33, 138
Redfin Fairy, 34, 139
Redtail, 157
Sixline, 34, 140
Smalltail Pencil, 159
Spanish Hogfish, 141

Benthic – pertaining to living on or near the sea floor or substrate.

Confamilial – a member of the same family.

Congener – a member of the same genus.

Consexual – a member of the same sex.

Conspecific – a member of the same species.

Detritus - decomposing organic particles, which include animal remains, plant remains, waste products and the bacteria and other microorganisms associated with it.

Dither fish – an active, bold fish that swims in the water column and gives more timid species the confidence to emerge from hiding.

Heterospecific – a member of a different species.

Motile – free-living, mobile.

Nano-reef – a reef aquarium that is smaller than 30 gallons.

Predator aquarium – a community tank that contains fish-eating species, such as lizardfishes, frogfishes, toadfishes, lionfishes, scorpionfishes, and groupers.

Protogynous hermaphrodite – a species that changes sex from female to male.

Protandric hermaphrodite – a species that changes sex from male to female.

Species or specimen aquarium – an aquarium dedicated to only one species or just a single individual of that species.

PHOTOGRAPHY

All photographs by
Scott W. Michael
except where indicated:

Alf Jacob Nilsen (Bioquatic Photo: biophoto.net): 12, 38, 58, 75, 86, 120, 121, 122, 168

Roger Steene: 35, 58, 126

Larry Jackson: 32

Janine Cairns-Michael: 192

PHOTO RESEARCH
Ryan Greene, T.F.H.

ILLUSTRATIONS
All Illustrations by **Joshua Highter**

DESIGN
Susie Forbes

COLOR
Digital Engine (Burlington, VT)

EDITING
**Judith Billard, Alesia Depot, James Lawrence,
Mary E. Sweeney, Kathleen Wood**

Scott W. Michael is an internationally recognized writer, underwater photographer, and marine biology researcher specializing in reef fishes. He is a regular contributor to *Aquarium Fish* Magazine and is the author of the *PocketExpert Guide to Marine Fishes* (Microcosm/TFH), the 6-volume *Reef Fishes* Series (Microcosm/TFH), *Reef Sharks & Rays of the World* (Sea Challengers), and *Aquarium Sharks & Rays* (Microcosm/TFH).

Having studied biology at the University of Nebraska, he has been involved in research projects on sharks, rays, frogfishes, and the behavior of reef fishes. He has also served as scientific consultant for *National Geographic Explorer* and the Discovery Channel. His work has led him from Cocos Island in the Eastern Pacific to various points in the Indo-Pacific as well as the Red Sea, the Gulf of Mexico, and many Caribbean reefs.

A marine aquarist since boyhood, he has kept tropical fishes for more than 30 years, with many years of involvement in the aquarium world, including a period of tropical fish store management and ownership. He is a partner in an extensive educational website, www.coralrealm.com.

Scott Michael lives with his wife, underwater photographer Janine Cairns-Michael, and their Golden Retriever, Ruby, in Lincoln, Nebraska.